From Trauma
to Triumph

From Trauma to Triumph
The End

Finding your way out

Rachael Kelly

Published by Game Changer Publishing

Disclaimers:

1. Please note the information contained within this document is for educational and entertainment purposes only. All effort has been executed to present accurate, up to date, and reliable, complete information. No warranties of any kind are declared or implied. Readers acknowledge that the author is not engaging in the rendering of legal, financial, medical or professional advice. The content within this book has been derived from various sources. Please consult a licensed professional before attempting any techniques outlined in this book. By reading this document, the reader agrees that under no circumstances is the author responsible for any losses, direct or indirect, which are incurred as a result of the use of information contained within this document, including, but not limited to, — errors, omissions, or inaccuracies.

2. This book was written by memory, and mine is imperfect. I've done my best to be faithful to my experiences, and when possible, have consulted others who were also present during that time.

Paperback ISBN: 978-1-965653-45-6
Hardcover ISBN: 978-1-965653-46-3
Digital ISBN: 978-1-965653-47-0

GAME CHANGER PUBLISHING
www.GameChangerPublishing.com

DEDICATION

To my boys, my true north, whose light and love I am so grateful for. You are beautiful, strong, amazing, intelligent, sweet, good human beings who remind me every day why it matters.

To other survivors and those still trapped in the cycles of abuse and trauma, there is a path to freedom. You can do it. You are enough. You are not alone.

To hurt people who hurt people, I hope this helps you to stop and heal yourself. You have the power to end the cycle.

To all the "Partners In Stability" out there. Thank you for your steadfast love, compassion, and understanding as we navigate recovery. You reflect to us the light within ourselves.

Thank you to everyone who played a part in helping me complete this project: those who helped and those who hurt. Both were a gift.

To Ryan, Richard, and male survivors of trauma whose story goes untold too.

Read This First

Just to say thanks for buying and reading my book, I would like to invite you to connect with us, no strings attached!

Scan the QR Code Here:

From Trauma to Triumph

The End

Finding your way out.

Rachael Kelly

GC GAME CHANGER PUBLISHING

www.GameChangerPublishing.com

Foreword

"When Opportunities to Stretch and Grow Present Themselves, Step into Them."

I will never forget the first time I met Rachael. I had just started at my first consumer brand company as the head of learning and development. I never worked in this industry before, and I was immersing myself in their day-to-day work, life, experiences, and challenges. Up came this well-dressed woman in crazy high heels with shockingly blue eyes that said, "I know what the fuck I am doing, so don't fuck with me." I also saw a need to be liked, to learn, to connect. I saw a willingness to love, to be vulnerable, to protect. I saw the hurt.

I knew we were destined to be friends.

For those who have experienced trauma, we know the draw we have to others who have similar scars. We see it behind the eyes, beneath the words, under the hard exterior. When we connect, it quickly becomes a bond; healthy or not, we will often run through fire for one another, even if we don't yet know each others' stories. There is a raw attachment that is inexplicably visceral, molecular even. We create space for each other; we listen with our hearts, with our souls.

To write one's trauma story and share it with the world is one of the bravest things we can do. No matter our role or the perceived permission we give, real or imagined, there is shame in letting others in. Survivors are brilliant at doing what we have had to learn: surviving. To do so, we have become adept at protecting ourselves, of keeping others away, of appearing threatening, of hiding so we are not seen. But, as with Kintsugi, the Japanese practice of repairing broken pottery with gold, these repairs are what make us stronger, are what make us special.

And like Kintsugi, Rachael's story and the lessons she has learned highlight how these fissures can be a beautiful gift. Through her raw narrative and vulnerability, she allows survivors to find that connection, to not feel alone and isolated in their experiences. In coupling that with her recovery journey and the things she has learned along the way, she provides insights and resources for healing. She allows her brokenness and her brilliance to help others and provides transparency into the rawness and wounds that are so often the underpinning of our drives and ambitions. She steps into the chaos with her hands held open, ready to walk beside us and provide stability as we move forward.

– Dr. Allessandria Polizzi

Table of Contents

PREFACE

Before we start, I want to say thank you for taking the time to read this book. It means a great deal to the hive that you've committed the time and energy to do so. I'd also like to explain how the book is structured. As we move through the conversation, I'll be speaking from three main perspectives: *storytelling*, current perspective, and scientific insights. The storytelling portion includes personal examples that are shared with the purpose of bringing to life insights and understanding about the cycles of trauma. I'll share what perspective I have now about those examples and incidents with the gift of time and reflection. And I'll share the relevant scientific element to this conversation, and in the examples shared. Included throughout are references and links to additional publications and sources you might find useful on the topic. This is housed through a landing page with all of the external content for your ease and reference in the future. Finally, as music has always been part of my journey and experience, it made sense to include it as I tell the story. I've created a Spotify playlist which can be found here: *https://open.spotify.com/playlist/6gcVvlM8sA1ZyqONLYq358*

Throughout the book, you'll see a music icon that looks like this with the number corresponding to the song on the playlist in chronological order:

Best wishes on your journey.

INTRODUCTION

Running. My first memory in life. I'm running up a steep hill. Heart pounding, breath rasping, petrified, faster and faster. Sweat dripping down my face as the hot sun burns my face. Pushing my legs down to take the next big step, harder and harder, as fast as I can possibly go at this age. Away from the playground behind me, down the hill at the end of a vast, green field. Running towards my small home at the top. The childhood home where I thought I would be safe: the crumbling walls of my bedroom, the musky, dark basement where I was violated, not for the first nor the last time.

Perhaps this memory is my first for a reason. As I reflect, I realize I've been running for my life all of my life—situation to situation, crisis to crisis, trauma to trauma—before finally breaking free. No one tells you this: When it first happens, while the cement is still wet, it eventually sets. That pattern is one you are doomed to repeat, effortlessly facilitate, and believe, with every fiber of your being, that you deserve. I don't want to keep running from pain anymore. I can't. I am frigging exhausted. It's time to breathe and exhale. It's time to find peace, focus on the boys and their journey, and support others in finding their own empowerment.

My aim in describing this journey is not to evoke pity or sympathy. My trauma is personal to me, and many people have overcome worse, more significant, more adverse circumstances to achieve far greater and far better than me. This is not to say that I am some superhero or amazing in really any way. In fact, that is precisely the point. I'm not. I have my own healthy list of flaws, failures, and regrets. I am human, just like you, regardless of what you see on my social media page.

I am sharing these experiences—dark, raw, hard, ugly experiences—because, as someone once wisely told me, "You gotta give it to keep it." I progress on my own recovery journey as I help others on theirs. The blessings I've received from others, often undeservingly and unknowingly at the time, have made a huge impact on my life. I feel compelled to share these blessings with others. This act of sharing gives my life greater purpose and meaning, making it worthy of these gifts. I share because when others see you openly walk through your pain, it can fuel their courage to face their own.

As we move through this story together, I've chosen examples from key phases in life that illustrate the cycles of trauma—what it does to a person and how it manifests in various ways. It is important to note that this is not for the sake of comparing severity or adversity nor to make statements about its significance. As I mentioned, we all experience trauma and pain in our hearts. We all find ways to cope with life and the challenges it brings. This is not about "dwelling on" or "holding on to" past pain. It's about illustrating the cycles that occur, understanding the science behind them, and sharing a path to breaking free and recovering. Along the way, I hope to offer insights into your personal journey, whatever it may be.

I hope there are things in this story that help you realize that any abuse or trauma for which you are shaming yourself is not your fault, nor something you should bear the shame for alone. Maybe these examples will spark a realization that none of us are perfect or innocent victims and teach you how to hold these truths together. Perhaps you will find a strategy to help you navigate your own experiences with big "T" or little "t" trauma. It might provide an insight that helps you become a better parent, lover, friend, or business leader to someone who has been or is in similar circumstances. After all, beneath everything, we all share in the experience and pain of humanity. Maybe it will be a shock and a giggle that is relieving because, let's face it, we need to laugh while we cry about some of this. But most of all, I am sharing to say that you are not alone. You do not have to do this alone. And you are enough. I promise.

PHASE 1

MINDFUCKED

CHAPTER 1

PIGTAILS

I started this recovery journey trying to figure out how to move past certain cycles and be the mom my kids deserve to have. I have to be healthy for that reason, if for no other, and it's on me to make that happen. What I found in that exploration, despite what a part of my mind fought against, was that the journey would have to go all the way to the bottom of the root in order to release its death grip on me. Failing to go all the way would enable it to grow back time and time again, as it always has. So, while the recovery journey didn't start here, it's where the healing begins, and so it's where we enter the story today.

I also need to share that what I remember from the early years is limited. I have more flashbacks than concrete memories. There are fierce protective parts within me that hold those walls up thick and heavy. Certain things I may never know. The precise events that started this chain reaction and the basis for these may always be scattered and fuzzy. That is okay. I don't need to know it all, I just need to release the grip.

I've pieced some things together between the things I remember, information from others, my own insights, and what happens during those flashbacks. The ones I've always had. While I am awake, while I am asleep, wherever in life I am, they find me. Pressure welling in my chest, heart pounding, frozen, restrained, petrified, violated, exposed, exploited, ashamed.

There is one particular memory that haunts me the most. I can feel large, strong hands, see eyes, feel pain and pressure in my body, hear myself scream with all my might with no sound coming out, falling into an endless black hole. The awful certainty that I am powerless, helpless, and on my own.

I can hear that voice in my head telling me that I am defective, repulsive, a fuck-up, a burden, a whore who should be ashamed of herself. But I don't know why. A voice tells me to shut up, be a good girl, put my head down, not to ask for anything or expect it. Reminds me not to get too big for my britches, to always remember that I don't deserve shit. But I can't tell who the voice is coming from. Later, I will try.

It is so frustrating to be unable to remember more: What gave me those sensations, where did those snippets of memory come from, and what truly lies at the bottom? But my parts and pieces staunchly protect that space, that person from so many years ago. They are fierce and unrelenting in their resolve to shelter and protect her and her pigtails. So for now, I recognize their presence, their need to exist, and I comfort her when they let me. I can validate and heal the impact without fully knowing which explosive caused the blast.

It was here that I first became a survivor: I learned how to compartmentalize and dissociate in the moment as it's happening. Later, I learned to disappear into fiction, consuming a book or two a day as soon as I learned how to read. I escaped into the world conjured in my mind, consuming each page like water in a desert. I disappeared into dance and music. When I could, I'd get away physically, finding a quiet space in the woods or somewhere no one could find me. But sometimes, my only escape was in my mind.

As I now share more about my parents, who were a key part of this stage, I acknowledge that parents are people, and people have the capacity for many different things, good and bad. There was a lot that was very good about what they did for me. They had their own difficulties and challenges they endured those years when I was a young child. There is no playbook for parenting, and they got a lot right.

I also know that while parents can do their best, hurt people hurt people. Hurt, *untreated* people become toxic, especially with their partners and children. Both were very human and had been traumatized in their lives without the tools or support to work through this in a healthy way. This was the Boomer generation, being raised by Traditionalists. There was no crying or complaining allowed. Emotion was equivalent to weakness. Skills were never developed. Wounds became unhealed scars.

We were very Midwest and barely middle class. Concepts of right and wrong, of caring for other people, of hard work, dedication, and sacrifice were part of that Midwest upbringing: being a good neighbor and going to church on Sunday.

There were good things—happy moments. Baking cookies and pies, arts and crafts, family pets, dance, summers at the pool. Good salt-of-the-earth Midwestern stuff. I know they wanted the best for us. They tried, providing what they could.

My father was the oldest of seven Catholic kids. His parents grew up during the Great Depression. They were poor—desperately poor—in rural Wisconsin. Their parents herding the kids like cattle, doing a number on their body, mind, and sense of boundaries. We suspect the priest sealed the deal by teaching them to surrender their bodies along with their spirit. But everyone was in church every week, smiling in their "Sunday best."

We don't know exactly what happened, and neither do they. We just experienced the fallout as it pulsed through all the branches of the family. That is the thing about the brain: When it needs to hide and protect certain things from you, it does. If you were to ask my father about his childhood, he would get a big smile on his face and describe something along the lines of an episode of Leave It to Beaver. *His ability to see and experience one thing and immediately view it as something very different from reality is a stark, stunning, and often detrimental survival skill he clearly learned early on. For us, growing up with a parent like that often had a profound gaslighting effect.*

My mother, who knows? She also views her early life as having been very rosy, very Midwest, yet exhibits a commitment to misery and unfulfillment in her own life. There is a reason people begin to demonstrate narcissistic victimization. I'll just never know the precise journey this particular pathology took. It preceded my existence by a long time. Nothing was ever good enough. There was always a reason to be in a state of emotional extremity. No one and nothing was ever able to make her happy—or not for very long, anyway.

In a way I empathize, as they had no clue how to love unconditionally and be present in an emotionally healthy way for children. How to care for their mind, body and heart. How to teach healthy boundaries and role model healthy relationships and self-love. They hadn't experienced that in their own lives. How could they possibly raise a healthy family? We lived out our destiny.

We struggled financially, always living with an undercurrent of instability and barely scraping by. Money was a constant source of stress, and we often felt inadequate. I was the middle child, embodying all the clichés associated with that position. Each of us had a unique experience growing up in that household. My younger brother's experience was probably most similar to mine. My sister, older by four years, would say she had a wonderful life growing up. Or perhaps that's the same coping mechanism—viewing things through rose-tinted lenses— that we learned so well from our dad.

For me, the experiences were marked by never, ever being good enough. There was extreme control, structure, and a demand for perfection in anything related to performance or image—whether it was church, school, sport, an outfit, or a smile in a picture. The message was always clear: Nothing was ever good enough, and we must always strive to be picture-perfect.

There was also something, an undercurrent, a feeling I can't quite describe. I don't remember exactly why. It's a pressure in my chest, a scream that builds but never escapes my throat. A feeling of uncertainty, always uncomfortable, walking on eggshells, a need to always protect my body, my mind, on guard for the next moment of powerlessness. It's a feeling that never leaves, it becomes more intense and acute during certain moments.

Regarding my mother, there was never enough appreciation or deference to validate her. She had a constant need for affirmation and appreciation, which extended far beyond us kids. Everything around her was negative: having to move away from her childhood area, the politics, the weather, something a company did or didn't do. There was always a reason to be unhappy. It was a relentless commitment to misery. No matter what we were doing, where we were going, or who was involved, it was bad.

I remember most holidays involving crying, miserable meals, and fights. Mother's Day was always the worst because we could never do enough to please her. One year, even the flowers I got her weren't good enough because they weren't her favorite. Within an hour of receiving them, she gave them to a friend. Small but significant. A million cuts, a million jabs, all the time. As a result, I came to be ingrained with a deep sense of never feeling good enough, always being a disappointment, and always being alone.

We learned to put on a very good public face. The skill of masking. Publicly, we were the perfect churchgoing, middle-class, Midwestern family. Professional parents, Dad was involved in teaching Sunday school and leading the "Wise Men's" club. Mom is a nurse by trade, always knitting or sewing something, including Halloween costumes, and making macaroni cheese and hotdogs for dinner. Today's equivalent would be "social media perfect."

My father loved the YMCA Indian Princesses program, which is intended to facilitate shared experiences for fathers and daughters. It included activities like making wooden race cars, camping, and earning feathers for their headdress. Activities the fathers wanted, not the daughters. My father went all out for it, loving the activities and the pomp and circumstance of the rituals. He wanted to be a group leader and act like a wonderful, committed, loving, fun dad. For me, seeing the public present so differently than what was true and real at home, being forced to smile, put on the mask, and pretend, hurt. Every moment felt like I was crazy. It was a lie, and I was powerless. I felt the pressure in my chest, my brain spun. I put on the smile as told.

At home, there was constant tension, anger, fighting, control, and unachievable expectations. It's hard to pinpoint the exact dramatic events that created this climate because it was all events. It was every day in every part of our life. Walking on eggshells in every action, comment, task. Immediate criticism and disapproval of all topics as a starting point. Ways to ensure there was always extreme control. A sleepover at my friend's house would often include the unexpected arrival of my dad to audit what we were watching, eating, or drinking. Suffering and sacrifice were considered character-building. If there was a way to do something in a more difficult rudimentary way, that was the path. Let's walk 5 miles through the city instead of driving. Push the lawnmower instead of motorized. Chop wood instead of a chainsaw. Cleaning was never clean enough and must be repeated multiple times, pushed well beyond the tears of a young child. Dishes never dry, polished, or shiny enough, A not an A+, hard work never hard enough, projects never done right enough. There are most certainly important lessons and skills built in these experiences. Taken individually, one might think those were even good lessons. It wasn't so much the individual thing, it was the collective, and the underlying aspect of constant power and control. It was the extreme, unrelenting, unachievable nature of how it was done. For a kid, militant and unrelenting control and lack of approval about every aspect of life, and every task performed, every project completed, every emotion felt, was deeply damaging. The public picture of family perfection and false narratives would ultimately come tumbling down.

CHAPTER 2

ELEMENTARY SCHOOL TORTURE

Through my elementary school years, we didn't have much money. I wore hand-me-down and discount clothes, but my sister and I had very different body types, so nothing really fit right. This was the 80s, with its horrible fashion. I had a bad "curly hair" haircut, super thick rose-tinted lenses in my glasses, and freckles covering my nose. I felt so uncomfortable in my own skin. I was also fairly intelligent and able to see and understand what was happening around me. I was shy, bright, introverted, creative, empathic, and sensitive. I lost myself in books a lot. Looking back, I think I can see some early signs of neurodivergence. I had overwhelming emotions and would quickly go from a peaceful state to a highly anxious one. I became deeply immersed in things that interested me and struggled with things that didn't. How much of that was ADHD? How much was anxiety? How much was PTSD? And how much was just being a normal kid going through the stages of development? It was likely a cocktail of all the above. I call it out because I didn't know until many years later that dysregulation and anxiety can be signs of ADHD, among other things. I had zero tools to deal with it and felt shame for what I was experiencing. Being around my father, I knew the rules: shut up, suck it up, push through, put on a good face. There's no crying in baseball. And above all else, don't talk about it.

I was prime picking for school bullying. Back then, there were no school policies or protections. It was old-school. It was the same group of people all those years—small town, small school. The class barely changed as we went through grade school. There was good, bad, and ugly within that group of kids. I would oscillate between having friends and being completely isolated and estranged. It showed up in so many ways throughout those school years. Who do you sit next to for lunch? Who gets picked for the team? Who gets picked by whom for project groups? And who is consistently left for last? Who is going to show up at my birthday party? Who am I going to play with? Especially cruel was the constant intentional social exclusion. All that shit. It's awful. One day I had friends to play and have fun with, and the next day, they turned and exploited my vulnerabilities. How I looked, my clothes, my hair, my glasses, or something I said or did, or something I was excluded from because I wasn't part of the crowd.

I remember walking home from school, kids circling me with their bikes, verbally humiliating me as I walked, trying to break me down through degradation. Tears ran down my face as I kept my feet moving, one after the other, just trying to make it home. Playing dodgeball in PE? Horrific. Not fun to be the kid everyone takes delight in targeting with the ball.

One of my most vivid memories is St. Paddy's Day in fifth grade. My dad's family went all out for St. Paddy's Day every year, especially my dad. It was a great opportunity to celebrate a façade and this Irish persona. I would always think to myself, I don't know why you're so proud of this. It's not like it's served you so well in life. *Our Irish Catholic heritage of abuse, shame, hiding, torment, dysfunction, and addiction—let's celebrate the heck out of that with some shamrocks and leprechauns, green clothing, and buttons everywhere. In my fifth-grade year, I was head-to-toe in Irish buttons, green clothes, makeup, and a hat. So much stuff that I walked in late, dressed for a St. Paddy's Day bar crawl, with all eyes on me, and no one else was wearing a thing. Oh my God. Like I needed another reason to be humiliated.*

Through these years of instability and pain at home, torment and uncertainty at school, I continued to experience big emotions I couldn't control. There was no safe place for me to process them, no safe place to be. So, I withdrew further inward.

I survived grade school. At the very end of it, my parents' marital problems escalated. I think my dad couldn't keep a consistent job. He was in sales, probably a commission-based role, hence the constant financial instability. As I vaguely recall, he may have tried to start a company. My mother worked two jobs while also going to school to advance her career. So, she was juggling school, three kids, and two jobs, working seven days a week.

My siblings and I were home alone with him on the weekends. It wasn't good: lots of fights and explosions because, as you may remember from our last chapter, there was extreme control. There were many house projects and responsibilities, and no such things as free time and space. I joke that the shows I watched as a kid were like L.A. Law and Miami Vice, not Saturday morning cartoons because I watched TV late at night. Saturdays were chores and demands, chasing him around all day, cleaning up after projects, polishing dishes perfectly, cleaning everything. There was no ownership of my own time or agency. As I got older, that tension escalated. A part of me started to fight back and resist the extreme control. That resistance became a battle of wills and conflict with my father. It exacerbated the issues in my parents' marriage because they didn't know how to parent me and couldn't align on how to respond. It traumatized my sister and brother because I was a spark in an already explosive marriage.

We started going to therapy. I saw the therapist alone, then my parents saw the therapist, and finally, we all went as a family. It didn't work: Therapy only works when you do the work and have the ability to self-reflect and make self-improvements, which neither of my parents was willing or capable of doing. I believe the last question the therapist asked my dad before he walked out was something about being like his father. That ended it—an interesting contradiction from the Leave It to Beaver upbringing.

Ultimately, the tension and fighting with my dad escalated into a final stand. We fought over sweeping the floor versus vacuuming the floor—a battle of control. I remember arguing with him in the hallway, and he exploded. He lifted me by the collar and hurled me to the ground, then started charging toward me. On my back on the ground, I hurriedly back-crawled into my room (thank God for swimming lessons). Heart pounding and head racing, I slammed the door shut and slid my dresser in front of it to keep him out. I was 10 years old. I started playing music on the boombox and turned up the volume. My heart was still pounding, and my mind was still racing. I opened the window, jumped out, and ran six blocks downtown to a payphone at Downers Grove. I don't remember it all that clearly—I was in full lizard brain mode, barely touching the ground. I know I called my mother and said, "I'm going to Robyn's, and I'm not coming back if he's there." I hung up the phone and made my way to her house. It wouldn't be the last time I made that trip to her doorstep.

Bill moved out, and he never came back—at least, not to live.

Now, obviously, I know that they certainly should not have been married, and I didn't cause their divorce. But back then, while I knew that in one sense, I also believed that I was the cause of the problems. In a way, I was. My sister and my brother certainly believed so, and I can understand why. I'm sure my shit caused trauma for them. The core belief I had of being defective, bad, shameful, awful went deeper and strengthened.

Now things start to get interesting. Again, I don't really have a clear memory, but I do know that I'm feeling abandoned. My mother is understandably a hot mess because she's now getting divorced, which isn't what she wanted. He left and chose not to come back. He tries to see us and wants to have joint custody. He comes over to the house to do projects, causing upheaval and continued conflict—like the time we didn't have a bathroom for a weekend with no advance warning due to an impromptu renovation. It was his continued way of exerting control and probably a way for him to spend his time.

Fast forward to me walking home one day after school, the last day of seventh grade. Susan picks me up and takes me to a hospital. I've been going to therapy, but for some reason, probably because I'm being a little bit rebellious, they thought that I was deeply depressed and in such a state that it warranted total medical intervention. Remember, I am bad and defective, so of course, such extremes are necessary. My mother is part of the hospital system where I go; she knew and understood the resources.

So I go to the hospital, and frankly, immediately, I feel a sense of relief. I was safe, and I could let my walls down and start to process the emotional backlog. I remember seeing other people who were there, hurting really badly. People my age who had tried to brutally hurt themselves. I wasn't trying to put a pencil in my vein. In a way, it was comforting and affirming to be around people who were even more messed up than I was. I think I probably felt like I was the normal one in the group. I embraced the treatment, discovering music therapy and art therapy. "I am a Rock" by Simon and Garfunkel—what great lyrics. I was not there for very long. I did the work wholeheartedly.

Family day came. My mother came, I think bringing my brother and sister. She did this part right. She got me health treatment, and for that, I am deeply grateful because I know what my life would have been like had I not received it. What I remember very clearly is that my father did NOT attend. Emotions and vulnerability are weak and unacceptable. People who experience emotion are defective. That was his toolset. So, family day is here. I call him and say something to the effect of, "Are you coming? Like, what the fuck?" His response was very cold, very clear: "No. This is your problem, not my problem." Message received loud and clear. I am bad, I am fucked up, I am defective, I am not worth it, and I should be ashamed of myself.

As these cognitions strengthen, they start to feel more natural and true. I believe it, even encourage or direct it sometimes, as a self-defeating way of confirming my own twisted truth. **I'm ugly. I'm stupid. I'm unwanted. I'm bad. I'm defective. I'm not worth it. I'm alone. I should feel shame.**

I don't start at the beginning of my life to lament about my parents or childhood and dwell in the past. I'm starting there because when doing the work, it is so important to look at those early years and understand the foundation that was set. The cement of your brain is still wet, and you are carving out the pieces and pathways of functioning, both good and bad. The significance and amount of human developmental processes that are happening here are important to recognize, as trauma, and especially repeated trauma, has a profound effect. It is the science of the matter. This is why I call the first phase of the journey "Mindfucked."

During this developmental stage, fundamental beliefs about ourselves and others are formed. Attachment styles are developed based on our experiences with our primary caregiver, and important cognitive, social, and emotional development occurs. After that, the cement hardens and sets. It's not impossible to change it after that, but you'd better bring one hell of a tool to do it.

Emotional and physical needs are a core part of a child's development and fundamental sense of self-worth. When a child's caregiver responds positively to those needs, the message received is, "I am worthy of love and care." When ignored or neglected, the cognition turns negative, such as, "I am not worthy of love and care." In my example, while certain physical needs were met with shelter, food, and clothing, the sense of physical and emotional safety was not, and at times, I experienced a sense of physical danger, powerlessness, and violation. The negative cognitions developed followed suit. The effect was profound and lifelong.

Attachment styles form in the first three years of life based on how a child's caregivers respond to their most basic needs physically *and* emotionally. Healthy attachment styles lead to happier lives, better relationships, better work performance, and better health than those who are unfortunate enough to fall in the other camp. For about 60% of the population, a secure attachment style is present. For the rest of us (and I suspect that number is increasing), we develop insecure attachment styles as a result of that gap.

Learn more about the science and your own attachment style.

SCAN THE QR CODE:

During that time, in my example, I developed a cross between a dismissive-avoidant and anxious-fearful attachment style. In other words, I would vacillate between being clingy and needy, on the one hand, and discarding and pushing away, on the other. The trauma neural wiring laid was:

- I am *never* good enough.
- I am *not* worthy of love.
- I'm *not* safe or secure.
- I *should* feel shame.
- I *am* powerless.
- I *am* alone.
- I *must* wear a mask.

This is what happens within the dynamics of a dysfunctional, toxic home. When parents who are wounded themselves carry that forward into future generations. When bad things happen and they're left unsaid.

The good news is that there are exciting and promising developments in science, neurology, and psychology related to this topic. Several of these helped me, and I'll share about them as we go. You have to face it, acknowledge what is there, and understand and appreciate how deeply entrenched in you it is. It is this kind of recognition, understanding, and awareness that enables you to dig all of it up and rewire it for good. Just like a weed, you have to pull it up by the root, leaving nothing behind. If you miss part of it because you rush, pretend a section isn't there, or don't treat it with appropriate seriousness, it will grow again and come back stronger.

CHAPTER 3

GLORIA DEI

Gloria Dei: the Latin for "Glory to God." Jump forward to junior high. The bullying has pretty much dissipated. Everyone is dispersed; we are in a much larger school now. I'm always worried about it happening again at any moment, even paranoid about it, waiting for the hammer to drop again. But it doesn't. I'm older now, and my mother has agreed to allow me to get contacts. Shedding the glasses was a big deal. I have pretty eyes, and people can now see me. I can also see better.

I'm starting to kind of discover myself a bit more, to emerge from my shell at school. I've discovered music, and I really escape into it, carrying that music therapy experience forward. It turns out I have a good voice. I join the choir at church and school, and start voice lessons after a while. I'm good. It's a beautiful escape. I'm feeling a little bit better.

I have a few friends–or people I'm friendly with (the distinctions are very precise at this stage of life). I also start to feel the attention of becoming attractive to others. I remember walking home from junior high, down the busy street, and people honking their horns. I remember the moment when I realized, "Wait a minute, you're honking the horn because I'm wearing a skirt, and I look cute. Am I attractive? Maybe I am desirable." It happened every time I wore a skirt.

This is a weird time, almost like a freefall. I'm not speaking with my father. He's totally gone now. My mother is battling through her own shit: getting divorced, losing her job, dating again. It's hard trying to take care of three kids as a single primary caregiver. She had a lot on her plate. I can appreciate how difficult it all was.

I'm receiving thorough training in Sunday school. In the Lutheran Church, you undergo confirmation into the Christian church during your junior high school years. You take a series of classes and retreats and activities; then, you go through a confirmation ceremony where you confirm your belief in Jesus and Christianity—the Lutheran version of Christianity. I'm going through these classes, and I'm in the choir. I'm going to church every Sunday, and I'm singing at all the services.

The class became the real challenge. I remember sitting there, thinking, This is a load of bull crap. *All the stuff they were talking about, essentially educating us on and wanting us to confirm. Please know, as an adult, I absolutely have deep respect for religion, its place, people's faith, and spirituality. I have my own. But at that time, it angered me.*

I thought to myself, "I know people like you standing up in front of class, preaching this stuff. I know what they are really doing at home."

Why? Because the church represented my father and his family and all of their hypocrisy, judgment, and shame. When you mixed that with my early teenage hormones and brain, it led straight to rebellion.

I would ask questions in a way that pointed out the contradictions and hypocrisy. I made a point of telling them that I didn't agree. But at the same time, I'd be in choir religiously, at every service like an angel. They had no clue how to deal with me.

I'm also at this age where boys are starting to discover their hormones, and I like the attention. We were too young; there was nothing sexual that happened in those years or in those relationships, but a group of us became rebel friends. It didn't help that the pastor's daughter was also in my confirmation class.

I think there were two things that probably caused this next event. They could force me to go to class and do the activities, but I was not going to stand in front of the congregation and confirm. They couldn't and wouldn't force me to do that. Just to make sure everyone was very clear about that, on our church retreat, I played "Stairway to Heaven" over the loudspeaker, so you know exactly where I was. I'm going to go into the woods, smoke some cigarettes, and talk some shit with the guys. I was a bit angry at this point, but fairly harmless: still a sweet, sensitive girl at heart, now just with a badass wrapped around her. We have multiple parts of ourselves as we experience life.

They did not like me, the pastor's daughter, and her friends. I was a young, independent, rebellious girl. I don't really remember having many exchanges with them, but I remember the looks, and maybe we did the middle school girl version of taunting and antagonizing. What I do know is that no matter how hard-ass I came off, I was a soft, gentle, sensitive girl at heart.

She made up a story that I had ripped her jacket off and tried to throw her down the stairs. It was a devastating lie. I remember my mother telling me this, and I remember feeling horrified that someone would think that, much less accuse me of it. It was behavior so antithetical to me. How could someone say that? Oh, wait: You mean the church people believe it?! I couldn't understand why, even with my stupid, rebellious harm, which up until that point I really thought was harmless and that someone would see through. I deserved to be punished and admonished for being an ass. But what I needed was someone to care enough to ask, "Why?"

There is a big difference between being rebellious and somebody exploiting the rebellious reputation I had created by inventing a complete fabrication with the specific intent of causing hurt. Not only did the leaders unequivocally believe this lie, but they also never even attempted to explore, investigate, or discuss it. They called my mother and said, "Hey, look, she does not want to be here, and you know what? We don't want her back." To which my mother agreed.

And with that rejection, on top of the others, I knew those early whispers to be true: You are worthless, you are defective, you are a whore, you should be ashamed of yourself. I am not worth understanding or caring about. I must just be completely awful.

I never set foot in church again. I didn't really miss church, obviously. I didn't miss the services. But I deeply missed the music. I ached to experience it again. I was really sad and felt very rejected and, once again, alone, as a result of my own doing.

As I reflect on the church experience, I think about the different types of betrayals that happen in life. There are toxic relationships and betrayals that happen with the person that you love and trust or that you think loves you. And then there are betrayals and traumas that happen with institutions that promise to be there for you, exist for a noble purpose, and espouse certain beliefs. It's not unusual for survivors who experience one kind to experience the other (feeling it more acutely than others), which becomes a reinforcement of the toxic internal narrative of worthlessness that has been sown. Institutional trauma amplifies and re-traumatizes while feeding and strengthening those narratives. This is where, as a survivor, you know that you are really on your own, without any power, fending for yourself. And you believe, you know, as your truth, it is exactly what you deserve.

CHAPTER 4

AGE AIN'T NOTHIN'
BUT A NUMBER

I'm starting to not feel like so much of an ugly duckling, but still do not really understand why people around me are responding to and treating me differently. I've spent the last couple of years without having been bullied by anyone at school, feeling stunned from what has happened at church, and I'm 13 years old at this point, in eighth grade. In the romantic arena, to date, I've had one boyfriend, with whom our shared activities were riding our bikes together and watching TV in the basement. I don't even think I kissed him. So, I've not really had a boy experience at all. Now, it's graduation week.

Graduation from junior high turned ugly when my updo and makeup job really upset my mother. Too womanly, too sexy, too suggestive. I don't remember the exact exchange. I just remember I was wearing a white dress, my hair up in a French twist, and I had makeup on. It probably stands out to me because my sense of beauty, self-esteem, appearance, and desirability was completely jacked up at this point. I was desperate for approval and validation, and the opposite cut like a knife.

On graduation weekend, my friend Robyn and I are alone at her house. We've been on-again, off-again friends since kindergarten. Robyn was never one of the nasty ones. She had her own set of shit and her own fucked-up family and traumas that she was just trying to survive. This is probably why we connected, even though, at the time, I didn't know it.

My mother's probably on a date or out for the weekend—I don't recall. It's Friday night, and Robyn's older sister is having a kind of "end-of-school," "end-of-year" party. We decided that we were going to crash this party. Of course, we wanted to be cool and sexy and hip. It's a bunch of older kids.

I'm sure we stood out as 13-year-old girls in the summer after junior high. I am sure I looked awkward: As I noted earlier, all my clothes were kind of awkward, discount or hand-me-down. Nothing ever quite fit right. In that sense, the outside matched the inside because nothing ever quite felt right either.

This is where I meet Ben. I remember him and his brother, who was an attorney (or so he said), being really interested in me. Looking at me with his deep brown magnetic eyes, with such interest and adoration and desire. Immediately, I'm flooded with a euphoric feeling.

At a certain point, he asked me to take a walk with him. My heart was pounding, and my head was racing: This man is really interested in me! I'm being seen, heard, and wanted. So we take a long, slow walk down Blodgett Street. It was a walk that I'd made a thousand times before, to and from elementary school, often in pigtails.

We walked down the street under the dim lighting of the streetlamps and the stars, a beautiful early summer evening in Chicago. I can't remember what we talked about; I just remember feeling happy and swept away. He held my hand as we kept walking. I could feel my heart leap out of my chest. Then, after a few slow blocks, he stops. Holding my hand, he pauses, turns, and kisses me under the stars. I had never been kissed like that before. I don't think I had ever been kissed romantically, ever before. Here was this man, this mature, smart, adult man, kissing me. A man wanted me. It filled me up, like what I imagine heroin feels like the first time a user shoots up. The gnawing pain that constantly consumed me was replaced with a warmth that swept over me like a gentle ocean wave.

I am immediately hooked. I know this is not right—I know he's an adult. Part of me was like, "Wait! What's going on here?" But the need for that hole to be filled overcame the resistance. Here was someone who saw value in me, who was interested in my thoughts, my feelings, and my dreams. He wanted me. I can't imagine what we talked about that night, and I don't remember what happened after that, but we made plans to see each other again. And we do just that. Immediately.

It's summertime. I have free time during the day. There is very loose supervision. This is the era of the latchkey kid. It's the summer before high school. I'm 13. My brother is 11. My sister, at this point, is 17, so she is off to college.

Ben and I would spend afternoons just lying in the park, having a picnic. It was magical. I couldn't get enough. I started making excuses and reasons to be gone longer and longer during the day, to spend that time with him. Eventually, we moved from the park, having picnics and watching the clouds, to his apartment, where we spent afternoons. At some point that summer, those afternoons turned into sex. I'm happy that he's happy and that I am causing it. I don't really like the act per se, but I'm hooked on the rush of his reaction to me. I quickly learned to surrender my body to him and to enjoy feeling good and validated that he was achieving enjoyment and doing things that pleased him.

That was the summer after my eighth-grade junior high year. I was 13. Ben was 23.

He was a 23-year-old man who had graduated high school and worked and had his own apartment and a beat-up old car. He had a scruffy face and worn hands. He was an adult, and he knew what he was doing. It's taken me a long time to recognize that reality. I still struggle with the feelings of responsibility I have for what happened, even though I know how incorrect that thinking is. That internal conflict, how your thinking and actions are manipulated, and the decisions that you make while under the influence of coercive control and grooming are really hard to come to terms with. I believed I was fully in control. I believed I was to blame. I did make certain decisions, after all. It's complicated. But I was also a child unable to make these decisions for herself. I was unprotected, defenseless, and, more importantly, prewired for predator grooming.

For so long, the narrative in our relationship, the belief I held in my mind, was that I was just so special, unique, and mature that, you know, he had inexplicably fallen in love with me, and we were meant to be together. Age didn't matter.

Age ain't nothin' but a number.

My friend knew about it. He used to be the neighbor; that's how they ended up at that party, him and his brother. Her mother knew about it, and I suspect that she was the one who gave my mom a heads-up about what was going on. Because one day, my mother confronted me. We got into a huge blowout fight, and she told me I could never see him again and that I needed to end the relationship. I was furious because, by this point, I could not imagine breathing without him. I would rather die than not be with this man. I was addicted to his "love" and attention. I don't recall exactly how our fight ended, but it wasn't good. Likely, it was an exhausted stalemate where we retreated to our respective corners for a break.

This was an important insight for me later in the awakening period when I reflected on my own maternal instincts and the knowledge I have today. I can't imagine standing by while a predator repeatedly rapes my daughter and doing nothing other than to tell *her* to stop the rape. That approach does not work. It will never work. This situation warranted law enforcement involvement, criminal charges, prosecution, and very close supervision.

There is no doubt I was a handful by this time in life: spiteful from pain, rebellious, and independent from necessity. A single mother of any kind would struggle with a strong-willed kid like me. A narcissistic mother will not put forth the effort, especially when the situation feeds her own victim narrative.

There are other reasons why the appropriate response didn't happen. From a societal perspective, we often blame the woman for her bewitching ways. We blame her sexuality, her appeal, her clothes, and her actions. We make her the reason, the scapegoat, that villain for the predator's predatory behavior. And we fixate on the victim's behaviors, to the exclusion of the predator. Hebephilia was somewhat normalized at that time, with pop culture images of adult men with young teenage girls. There was plenty of material to help justify what was happening. There are probably people who will read this story and have a similar reaction and judgment. These situations can be really confusing and uncomfortable to people. That's part of why they stay in the dark.

It took a long time for me to be able to recognize and examine this time period with an open heart and mind. The shame gripped me for so very long I couldn't bring myself to see. Decades.

I connect with him and tell him what is going on. His response is to withdraw. I reacted very poorly because, at this point, I'm completely hooked. I beg him not to end the relationship. I plead. At this point, I think I'm completely in love. I think that this is the person I need to spend my life with. I'm desperate. I cannot imagine not having him in my life. I walk 15 miles to his apartment and show up on his doorstep. I am as determined as I am misguided. So he says, "Okay. We are meant to be. We are soulmates. Age isn't relevant to our love; that's pure. We just have to figure out how to work within the system that exists so we can be together." So we devised a plan.

I can get emancipated at 15. So we just need to make it through the next couple of years until that time. The first step is to pretend that I'm no longer seeing him. Eat the shit sandwich. Make her think she has won. My mother's never met him. She doesn't know what he looks like. The summer is almost over. I am about to start high school. We can manage to get through a few weeks, getting only a few moments together here and there when we can. It will be hard, but we can manage. In a few weeks, we can introduce him as an older teenager from school. We craft the plan and start to put it into play. And it works.

A few weeks later, when I start to introduce him, she accepts it. I spend the next three and a half years living a dual life. My close friends at school know what is going on. But I'm also becoming a little more isolated from them. I'm in the choir. I try a couple of other extracurricular activities, but he doesn't really want me doing any of those things. He doesn't want me to have close friends. He doesn't want me to go to kid parties. So I don't, because I don't want to disappoint him, and I don't want to have a fight. Because when we fight, my room becomes destroyed, he punches holes in the walls, and smashes my personal effects. I'm screamed at, and then I'm discarded.

I don't want to displease him. He would provide things, and then he'd destroy them. Or he'd provide them, and then he'd take them away. Always in anger during a fight. And the fights were constant.

There were seemingly calm times. It was important then to keep things calm, not do anything to upset the applecart, make him happy, and spread my legs on the sofa under the blanket when he wanted. I could just lay there and pretend to watch TV.

The gifts came in again, the stuff, things I had never had because we were poor. It was exciting; I was special, he loved me, and he was taking care of me. And inevitably, the anger followed. What the one hand giveth the other taketh away. And pretty soon, all the things were stripped away, and what remained was a bloody mess of smashed and broken pieces of things that used to be important to me strewn across my bedroom. Holes in the walls. Face swollen and crying. Consuming pain in my chest, bleeding out, destroyed, empty, unable to think anymore, not understanding what I had done wrong this time.

My social life was with him and his older brother, sometimes his mother and his brother's girlfriend. I was pretending to be a girl in her early 20s. His brother knew. During the day I was a shy teenager again, keeping my head down at school for the most part. I got really into vocal music. That became my escape. I started to take voice lessons. I was in the choir. I was in the ensembles. It was cathartic.

At home, my mother is pretty much gone most of the time. She's dating, and then she meets a man she falls in love with, and they're gone all the time. Most weekends, they have an adventure somewhere. He travels for work, so she would go with him on trips. So much so that, at one point, one of the adult babysitters literally said to her, "Hey, maybe you should be around your kids more because they need you." But at that point, my mother had already given me and my brother the speech, "Hey, I spent the first part of my life taking care of you. Now I'm going to take care of myself. I'll make sure you have food. I'll make sure you have the basic things that you need, but I need to focus on me now."

She hadn't had it easy, not by any stretch of the imagination. So, part of me understood her need to prioritize her own needs so much farther ahead of ours. We knew we were mostly on our own. It became the perfect space for my "boyfriend" to come in, to control, and to really consolidate the cycles of abuse. It just happened to be accompanied by a willful, blind ignorance as to what was actually going on.

She gets remarried. There's a lot of tension between the kids on both sides, and both parents. It's really dysfunctional and angry. His kids are messed up and have issues from their own upbringing and experience in life. It was this really weird time for this dysfunctional family that became a dysfunctional blended family with messed up people and these deep, deep, painful hidden secrets.

I was simultaneously in that constant cycle with Ben, and it escalated. He would get more and more displeased with things that I would do. If I became more confident in anything or achieved anything, that would trigger an explosion, a devaluation, and a rejection of me. Things like a solo in a choral performance, or winning an award, or even getting invited to a party.

At a certain point, we bring my brother into the secret of who he really is, and he starts to become aware of the duality.

There was an inner voice. Over time it spoke louder, providing some inner resistance to what was going on. You really learn to shush that voice and ignore it in these toxic cycles, but it was there.

I hit senior year, and I had a real sense of loss. This period of my life was almost over, and I had missed so many experiences and so many close friendships. I longed for those goofy, carefree, shared experiences that high school kids have. On New Year's Eve, Ben really wants to go downtown. I really want to go to my friend's party. We get into a huge fight. He explodes and trashes my bedroom, like always. For some reason, this time is my breaking point.

I kick him out and ask my friend Becky to come and get me. Arriving at my house, she takes one look around and says, "Come with me. We are outta here." I don't remember much from the rest of that night, but I think I found myself being comforted by someone in one of the beds in her house.

After this, I'm in this kind of freefall, and he won't leave me alone. He won't stop calling me. He shows up unannounced. He sneaks into my room and slips into my bed at night, as he had done so many times before, only this time clearly with no consent. In retrospect, it took a lot of guts: a 27-year-old man sneaking into a 17-year-old girl's room in the middle of the night, her parents down the hall. He calls me drunk. Shows up drunk. He won't stop.

Now the walls start to cave in, and I'm afraid for my safety. I can't control it. I can't stop it. I'm helpless. I'm afraid.

I go to my mother and confess it all. Her response? Anger. "How could you? Like, how could you lie to me? How could you do this? How could you? How could you? You should be ashamed of yourself." I call Ben's mother to beg her to intervene with him and get him to stop. Her response? "You're a horrible human, and you've hurt my son."

After that, things became a haze. I stopped participating. I was a really talented singer, and I had a fairly promising music path in front of me. I started smoking cigarettes to hurt my voice. I allowed my body and my mind to continue to be exploited. I was really familiar with that. It was numbing. I would even invite it in, seek it out—anything to numb a certain pain and gaping hole that was still there.

It was hard for my friends. What do you do when you're a teenage kid, and your friend loses her mind and starts acting totally different than what you've known? Especially when you have your own trauma. So, most of my friends didn't want to be around me or have anything to do with me. I learned later on how my friend Stacy, not even knowing what was going on, fought back against the vicious rumors. She was an advocate then, and it's no surprise she is an advocate now. My new friend Becky stuck with me, I think because she understood. She was going through her own trauma triage and coping, and she understood the torment that I was experiencing.

I threw away my college aspirations. My vocal partner betrayed me, a girl who had been a really close friend for many years. We sang complementary parts and had a beautiful, combined sound with our different vocal tones and textures. Some of my favorite music memories were in those rehearsals. She, like the others—including teachers and vocal directors—started to distance themselves, giving me that look that said, "We know you're a failure and a fuck-up." And once that assessment was made, forget it, it's not worth the effort.

My mom did give me mental health help. I continue to go to a therapist. I spent a few days in treatment, but I just can't stop the self-destructive cycle. Like any drug, you develop tolerance and have to increase the dosage to maintain the effect. So, I continue to elevate my game and use it to numb the deep pain and torment consuming every part of my body. It gripped my chest every second of the day, the knife twisting slowly in the wound as I did things to facilitate my own exploitation and destruction. I am easy prey at this point.

I was drawn like a moth to a flame. It became my first glimpse into human trafficking. I didn't realize I was becoming one of the statistics.

These were the early days of the internet. Dark offices, rooms, and hidden cameras. I connected to him through a woman at work. It was all a haze. Between the drugs I was prescribed, the pain raging inside, and the weed I was starting to smoke, my 17-year-old brain wasn't functioning well.

I would go to his office, downtown Chicago, late at night, park my car, and slip inside this tall office building somewhere near Michigan Avenue. We never went anywhere but that dark, cold, office with hard carpeting he would take me on. Yet I believed that we were going to be together. That he would pick me up someday from my house, in his beautiful car, and we would be off, enjoying life. It's called "future faking." I'm certain cameras caught and broadcast those encounters. I shudder to think what kind of money he made. Deception, manipulation, exploitation, doctors office, and finally, the inevitable discard. I never hear from him again.

A path I seem to find myself, on the edge of a darker world of people. Some part of me instinctively knows where this leads. But by this time, I am completely on my own, untethered, lost.

My mother kicks me out of the house. Garbage bags of clothes on the front porch. Locks changed.

I am hopeless, homeless, worthless, and alone.

At the time Ben finally disappeared, I thought something had been done legally to intervene. But it turns out that wasn't true. He disappeared from me because he had moved on to my brother. I don't know everything that occurred. My brother told me that he never had sexual interactions with him. I'm not sure I believe that. Regardless, there were deep boundary violations.

He would sneak into my brother's room in the middle of the night and sleep next to him in his bed. Keep in mind my brother's bedroom shared a wall with my mother's. At that point, this was a 28-year-old man sleeping in bed next to a 16-year-old boy. They started to take excursions to the city on the weekends. In fact, he was around my brother so much that one of the weekends that my mother was gone, my sister found him, called the police, and had him removed from the premises.

No other intervention happened until several months later when an event finally triggered some action. Around 3 a.m. one night, my mother woke up to find Ben standing in her bedroom, looking at her and her husband. He said to her, "I am every parent's worst nightmare." As if in a plea to finally do something to intervene. Finally, she contacts the police and gets an order of protection.[1]

This example, this story, is so very painful to tell. I was not an *innocent* victim, but I was still a victim. It's such a powerful example of how children fall through the holes in society, how predators groom them and strengthen the cycle, and how powerful the cycle is. An adult man sexually interested in an early pubescent girl is called hebephilia. It is a strong and destructive form of abuse.

There are accounts of R. Kelly, the R&B artist, talking about his inappropriate, abusive relationship with a 14- or 15-year-old girl when he was an adult man. (It's worth remembering that he wrote a song called "Age Ain't Nothing But a Number.") There are reports of R. Kelly scanning a room of young girls and being able to identify in an instant those most vulnerable to his methods. There is a special set of skills these particular predators develop and use so brilliantly.

Aaliyah was 14 when she wrote this song with R. Kelly. At 15, she married him in secret.

Let's talk about the science behind what was happening here.

One of the aspects of the cycle at play here is coercive control, trauma bonding, and Stockholm syndrome. These methods are key

---

[1] This is based on what I've been able to gather about the events since then, not having been living at home at the time.

aspects of sexual abuse cycles perpetuated by abusers who live in the dark triad. It's extremely difficult for individuals who have not experienced this type of abuse to understand, especially because it is entirely invisible and seemingly within the control of the victim, who is very much under the psychological control of the abuser. It is a form of mind control that uses neurological conditioning, chemical processes (and addiction to those processes), and force to get the victim to behave in ways the abuser wants them to. The victim suspends their own reality for that laid out by the abuser and the abuser's voice telling her what she needs to do. It creates a cognitive dissonance that later becomes important to remember. The concept of coercive control answers the questions outsiders might have, such as:

- How could you stay?
- Why don't you leave?
- Was he physical?
- What did you do that may have provoked him?
- Did he hold a gun to your head?
- Didn't you know what you were doing or what you were getting yourself into?

It can be difficult to grasp how people can allow themselves to be dragged into such situations if one does not understand the compulsion and the pull of that addiction.

In addition, victims in this stage are not their best selves, hence my comment about not being "innocent." They are dysregulated, hyper-aroused, off-kilter, acting out, and self-destructive. When a predator taps into existing neural pathways and then continues to twist and strengthen them for their own benefit, the victim's behavior is easily orchestrated in a certain way. It is the science of it.

The addictive nature of what is happening is akin to a drug addiction. In many ways, that is exactly what it is. Oxytocin (the love hormone) and dopamine are released in the brain, dispensed, and controlled by the abuser in the cycle. Those are both powerful forces being used to control behavior. It is why, in this example, when I was with him that first time with a gaping hole of pain, I felt that rush, that warmth, that wave wash over me, and I was hooked. When he looked at me or kissed me, I could feel him just pouring into that hole. Oxytocin, the "Love Hormone." Then the reward, dopamine, comes for doing the things they want you to do. Control? Easy. Threaten to withdraw or begin to do so; then I'll really sing for my supper. Predators are drug dealers of the worst kind. That's the addictive nature of the cycle and explains why victims aren't thinking clearly. For me, it all continued to set the stage for my next act in life.

Read more about the science behind these concepts.
SCAN THE QR CODE:

This is also where the science of neurology, psychology, and sociology start to intersect. There is a long-term effect of what is called Adverse Childhood Experiences (ACEs). The level of impact is directly related to the severity, number, and frequency that a human being experiences of these ACEs during childhood. "Preventing ACEs could potentially reduce many health conditions. Estimates show up to 1.9 million heart disease cases, and 21 million depression cases potentially could have been avoided by preventing ACEs." The impact on our health and families is significant. What about those who are well past the time of prevention and are grappling with those long-term effects? This is an important question to ask ourselves. The population is not small. Trauma does not discriminate; it crosses every demographic.

According to the Centers for Disease Control, "ACEs are common. About 64% of adults in the United States reported they had experienced at least one type of ACE before age 18. Nearly one in six (17.3%) adults reported they had experienced four or more types of ACEs. We see the ripple in the rise of mental health issues. One in ten Americans have been diagnosed with a major mental health condition in the last five years. And the impact on society and our economy continues to ripple while organizations and institutions work across the world to triage the problem. The US Surgeon General and the World Health Organization have identified mental health as a top priority. According to the Society for Human Resources Management, half of employee disabilities are related to mental health. Trauma-informed care and leadership are sweeping through healthcare and education to enable their teams to take care of patients and lead employees. The line connecting early childhood trauma, the long-term health of that human being, the impact on our healthcare system and society, and the need and benefit to support survivors in their journey could not be more clear.

Learn more about Adverse Childhood Experiences and their implications here.
SCAN THE QR CODE:

And for survivors, it's time to give our experiences the space and grace necessary to process their impact, appreciate their effects, and truly break free. The coming chapters will discuss what happens when we don't.

Phase 1: Reflection and Journaling

As you reflect on the insights from this first phase, there may be things in there that resonate with you or that don't. And you may have questions about how some of this stuff can happen. I encourage you to pause for a moment and think. A thorough grasp of this part of the story is key to being trauma-informed and understanding the role of childhood development in the abuse of minors. These sorts of interpersonal situations are complex. While a child or a teenager has intellect, some agency, and knowledge of right and wrong, this doesn't mean they have control of their actions or the ability to make good decisions. I certainly did not. If you experienced anything like this and feel shame and guilt for it, it's time to let it go. It's not your fault: You didn't deserve what happened to you, and you are not alone. It's not your burden to carry. Healing involves understanding, forgiving yourself, and moving forward with resilience. Your past experiences can shape you, but they do not define you.

I encourage you to take a moment to read a little bit more about the four attachment styles and to take one of the free quizzes to get a sense of your own approach. Think about your early life experiences with your parents or your primary caregivers from the first few years of your life. What were those relationships, and how were you cared for both emotionally and physically? What were those gaps? It's okay to acknowledge where the gaps are and experience anger or sadness while also loving and appreciating the caregiver. Relationships are not one-dimensional. It's not about passing judgment on that person, just as it's not about avoiding accountability for yourself and your own actions. It's about assessing, acknowledging, and understanding your core so that you put yourself in a position to do something about the parts that need to change.

Journal Exercise

Take a moment to record in the journal section for this first phase in your life, the early formative years:

- What key early childhood experiences occurred?

_____

_____

_____

_____

o   What self-cognitions or neural pathways (positive and negative) do you carry with you as a result?

_____

_____

_____

_____

o   How do those manifest in your life today (either positively or adversely)?

_____

_____

_____

_____

• What is your most likely attachment style?

_____

_____

_____

_____

_____

_____

_____

o   How does that show up in your professional and personal relationships?

_____

_____

_____

_____

o   How did those situations have a longer-term effect on your life, health, and relationships?

_____

_____

_____

_____

COPING

CHAPTER 5

NOT ME

I now go into a period in my journey where I'm just coping. I'm trying to survive. I came home to my things in a plastic garbage bag and did not have any place to go, but at least I had a job. I was working in a restaurant, and I had just begun an affair with another man—20 years older than me this time. I went to him for help. He had a beaten-down, abandoned, almost uninhabitable apartment above a neighborhood bar in Joliet, Illinois, about a mile from Statesville Prison. Think Blues Brothers. It was the place where the barflies downstairs would go to get high or have sex. There's electricity and running water (but no heat) and a mattress. At some point, somebody painted the walls white, and there were hardwood floors, but they didn't do a very good job, and they didn't cover it. So there were specks of white paint all over the floor. The front entryway was boarded up, so I would walk around the dimly lit back of the building and up the stairs through the back door.

I take my plastic bags, along with a blanket and my cat, and I begin to crash in this apartment. It's really dangerous. It's fucking Joliet and dark, and I'm working crazy hours now. I'm just trying to forget I exist. I'm working as many hours as I can to get overtime. I like the achievement-orientation of working in a restaurant. It's consuming me; it consumes my mind. There is a rush every day, and there are other degenerates like me: We're all rejects and societal misfits working at a pizza joint.

I would come home in the middle of the night and park my car down the street because nobody was supposed to know I was in this place. Then, I would walk down the street, around the back entrance, and walk up the stairs to the back door. At night I would wash my uniform in the kitchen sink. On payday, I would cash my check at the grocery store and get groceries. That was the highlight. The rest of the time I was usually eating pizza for my meals.

One day, I came home at two o'clock in the morning. I'm tired. It's probably been a 16-hour day. I walk in the door and into my living room, where I find tall crackhead Jimmy. I'm like, "Holy shit, what the f#ck are you doing here?" I can tell I startled him, and he's all jittery. Jimmy is a tall, skinny white guy with a gaunt look and burnt, blistered lips from the crack pipe. I'm scared, my heart pounding, and my lizard brain kicking in. "Jimmy, what the fuck are you doing here?!" He's jumpy and jittery. He gets down on the floor and starts scratching around. I'm like, "Excuse me, Jimmy, what the fuck are you doing here?"

And he says, "I dropped my rock." He's frantically scratching the floor, searching for the crack rock that he dropped and couldn't find among the old paint splatter. Oh my God, that was definitely rock bottom (if you'll pardon the pun).

Leveraging every source of influence I can think of, including calling my boyfriend, threatening the cops, and perhaps letting my inner warrior show her face, I finally convince him to get out, and he leaves. That was the moment I realized, "Holy fucking shit, this is not going to be my life. I am not doing this. I am not going to be around this." Something in me said, "No fucking way, not me."

For restaurant industry staff, there's a near-zero barrier to entry and high turnover, but it's sustainable because people always need to eat. At this time, hourly employees started at minimum wage, so people were always struggling to survive. It was mad chaos, but I saw an opportunity in it.

I started to see that I was part of this huge global company. I started to see the career paths. I went after lifting myself up with every ounce of energy, focus, and drive that I had within me. I sought mentors, learned and trained, and I took on every challenge to prove that I could accomplish it.

I advanced a lot. I had stumbles, for sure. But I worked my way up in the organization through every position and became a multi-unit leader. Then, I found my true passion. This is where my love of human resources, people, and culture came in. I fell in love with empowering people, helping them, giving them the systems, coaching the leaders and all the stuff around it, and harnessing human potential into business results. Helping other people with their social mobility fueled me so much because now I was able to do some good. I'm very lucky to have mentors who translate that passion into knowledge, skill, and accomplishment.

I worked really hard and continued to advance using the skills I learned. I used some of my survival skills and energy. That period was a blur, but it is really where I learned how to channel the energy of pain into something productive. For me, that was work. Never feeling good enough kept me humble and hungry, always pushing to prove myself. So, I was always getting better and enhancing my skills. It drove performance and enabled me to break through in so many ways. The industry I was in took it: they'd take everything I was willing to give because there was always a need. That dopamine from achievement became my drug. It never lasted long enough. Once I got through one promotion or achieved one thing, I always needed to go after the next because the buzz from the accomplishment never lasted very long.

During this time, I wasn't really solving that gaping hole. I was just coping and covering it and putting patches on it. Given that I have a touch of ADHD, I think restaurants and learning operations were great early professional training for my brain. I compartmentalized a lot. I put that shit on a fucking shelf and locked it away. Forgot that it existed. In a way, it was like a different life, a different person, not who I was anymore. I put it away and used the dysfunctional energy it gave me in a productive way.

The example of my career path, in this context, isn't about the unusual, remarkable, and fortunate nature of that aspect of my life. In this context, it's about sharing the example as a point of hope, resilience, and relatability. For survivors reading this, I want you to know and see that those in leadership roles are not so unlike you. This also means that you, too, have the same capacity to use your pain in a productive way. The things that happen to you do not have to define you. So easily, my life could have taken a very different course in so many ways, and I would not have been in a position of empowerment to break free when and how I did later on. I share the example of my career to say we aren't so different, you and me. I don't want you ever to see yourself as inadequate because of the ways those experiences impacted your life, both the initial impact and its ripple. You most certainly are enough.

The trauma neural wiring I outlined earlier served me well in some ways during this time. It helped me to advance. Those childhood weekends full of work and control became work ethic and perseverance in a chaotic, chronically understaffed, difficult environment. The use of my hands to do things became hands that could operate a business. My need for affirmation was channeled into a continuous striving for substantive contribution, improvement, learning, and growth. I connected so well to those leadership principles because they were so aligned with my wiring. I turned a situation in which nothing was ever enough and nothing was ever stable into a ceaseless striving for excellence.

This was the upside of my experiences. The key was learning that the things that are often great strengths can also become weaknesses. For example, in the coping stage, dissociation from the events and repressing pain and shame can lead to overindulgence in those strengths and unhealthy mechanisms to numb, fill, patch, and solve for. Ultimately, those mechanisms become poison. The box you've put things into leaks over time, and then you have a really contaminated mess.

Phase 2a: Reflection and Journaling

It is normal to put some distance between ourselves and difficult experiences while we soothe ourselves, lick our wounds, and try to move on. Grin, bear it, suck it up, and move on, so to speak. It's impossible to function in life without resilience—and it's miserable. Not all coping mechanisms are bad or harmful; sometimes, they can be very beneficial.

Journal Exercise

- Take a few moments and reflect on your own trauma coping mechanisms. What are yours?

_____

_____

_____

_____

- How do your coping mechanisms coincide with your preferred attachment style?

_____

_____

_____

_____

- How do you sometimes mask what's truly going on with a different "fix"?

  _____

  _____

  _____

  _____

- What have you already turned into fuel to power?

  _____

  _____

  _____

  _____

- What might start to burn you if you don't manage it?

  _____

  _____

  _____

  _____

CHAPTER 6

TOO GOOD TO BE TRUE

I've started to achieve certain things from a career standpoint. I've achieved what feels to me to be a really monumental and important promotion, which was really moving into the more professional aspects of operating a brand, and I'm no longer working in a restaurant. It's my first HR and training role. Despite the voice in my head loudly insisting, "I'm not pedigreed because I threw away my life and I didn't go to school, and so I'm a piece of shit who is going to be flipping burgers for the rest of my life," I charge forward in life and love.

I was in a relationship that I decided to exit two months before the wedding. I handled that breakup so poorly. While the breakup was the right thing to do, I regret hurting him and regret the way I left. We had been through some things together, including a tragic motorcycle accident 18 months earlier, with a long and tough recovery that we got through together and strong. But I was young. I had never lived life. I had no idea who I was. And if we had married, I'm confident I would have broken his heart worse. He dodged a bullet when I called off that wedding.

After I broke up the relationship for good, I moved to downtown Chicago, where I was sleeping on a roommate's couch. I started to bump up against the kind of life that I had barely given myself permission to even dream of hip, *modern city life, non-conforming to the heteronormative, Midwest, and religious expectations. F*ck them.*

Out one night with my girlfriends in downtown Chicago, in a crazy club, I meet the most perfect, amazing, sexy, worldly man who checks all of the boxes: artistic, intelligent, business-minded, Latino—everything I could want. We begin a whirlwind, intense romance that runs hot and cold by turns.

There would be intense, grand gestures and dramatic romantic moments. And then cold emotional distancing. Then, pull back in. This was the beginning of the cycle. I just thought this was a broken man who had been damaged from his prior relationship and that I was strong enough to solve it. I was by no means a perfect human myself. I was raw, intense, and mostly a mess in life. I can point to a million failures and flaws I had at that time, too. I was reactive and jealous but also independent, amazing, sexy, and sweet. I had my own dichotomy happening.

I foolishly thought I was the one to "fix" him. Apparently, I hadn't heard the lyrics of a million songs written about how you can't "fix" anyone but yourself. About a year into the roller-coaster relationship, anytime something big was going to happen, there would be some explosion. For example, the night before I was going to move in, it was, "Should we really do this?" Shit like that was happening all the time. He introduced an alternative relationship structure as a potential solution to the power struggle. We started to experiment with it. There was lots of trial and error.

A couple of years in, this led to triangulation with another woman who was deeply interested in him and "helping him with his art." There was an inappropriate emotional relationship that developed and was used to facilitate jealousy and drama. We were living together at the time. The strategy worked. I was stressed at this time with my father's mental breakdown, my job and responsibilities, and I was still early in my career. I was also in a new world and increasingly feeling insecure about my lack of pedigree. I acted out, eaten alive by my insecurity and jealousy. I was, of course, branded as being unreasonable and unjustified in my reaction. This was an early "crazy-making" scenario.

As the experimentation on our relationship structure continued, a part of me really resisted it. I would succumb to pressure, then retract and create a bad energy around it all. The pressure was always there. I was often reminded of what was in it for me, and there was certainly a benefit to me in doing so. I would try it at times, and there would be an explosion. I wasn't doing it right or doing it well enough. I didn't really want to do it. It was really dysfunctional. Sometimes it went right, and I started to learn how to have fun, relax, get into the vibe, and enjoy myself.

On the outside, we were this perfect couple. Professional, contemporary, doing these fun things and fun trips and growing in our relationship. Much of that was true; there were many happy moments, trips, experiences, and memories. Amazing experiences in many ways that, for a girl like me, I never thought would happen.

Several years into our relationship, through those ups and downs, slows, breaks, and reconnection, we became engaged. We had a beautiful wedding, full of joy and happiness, maybe a sense of relief of having made it through, starting a new chapter, and the anticipation of a beautiful, classy, and meaningful life. I felt beautiful and happy. I felt real joy. It was picture-perfect.

I even became a rock for my sister and brother during this time. I reconnected and strengthened the relationships with my sister and my brother, and they moved downtown as well. We were all spending time together, doing Sunday night dinners, and feeling like this family that I never, ever had. It felt good to be the center, the rock of that family, which was certainly not my reputation before then.

While all this is happening, my anxiety and depression, despite my career continuing to progress, are increasingly gripping my mind and heart. I'm still really struggling. Anxiety starts to leak and show up in work situations or in fights that he and I would have, creating a pattern of energy cycling. At the same time, I am having these amazing life experiences: buying a home, going to the Caribbean, enjoying beautiful things, beautiful friends, and all the stuff that looked perfect.

It just didn't feel perfect. It wasn't real.

Looking back, I see the cycle starting from the very beginning. I can see the pattern all the way through the relationship. It doesn't start out in the extreme. It starts very, very subtly. And like a steady, small trickle of water running down, it creates a pathway. It's not the first time the water has trickled down that this permanent pathway happens. But over time, it cuts a channel. That's the grooming part and the nature of the cycle. And I was going into it pretty well fucking trained. It all felt familiar.

There's a reason that survivors often have multiple cycles of toxicity. We internalize it as our fault, believing we're the ones who caused it. In some ways, we do even seek out or are drawn to those relationships. That's what we know. It's our reality. We are still seeking that oxytocin/dopamine cycle.

Here is the part that is critical to understand: Both truths can be held together. We may invite it in, seek it, and be drawn to these sorts of relationships; it doesn't mean that is what we deserve. It doesn't mean that sense of worthlessness is real. That voice constantly reminding you what a complete piece of shit you are is not right. It's trauma wiring and the addiction to the cycle. It's vital to understand that nuance and giving yourself compassion are key to changing your own behavior to stop it.

This is part of the mindfuck of the cycle: the sense of truth or accuracy of the negative cognitions *I am a worthless whore, I am bad,* whatever it may be. When it happens over and over and over again, you absolutely believe you deserve it and that you are indeed [insert negative cognition]. The predator tapping into that pre-existing wiring and strengthening it for the victim is reinforcing that trauma wiring. And at a certain point, already unwittingly deeply entrenched in the cycle, you embrace it all as your truth, and it becomes a self-fulfilling prophecy.

CHAPTER 7

THE GODDESS

A couple of years after we married, we moved from Chicago to Texas. It was a big shift for my family and hurtful to my brother, which I will always feel bad about. The move gave me some healthy distance from some things and was a massive life shift. There was a sense of leaving my past life and beginning a new one, starting where I was at that moment. It was surreal. We started with a new set of friends and colleagues, a big house in the suburbs, and a fun and cultured lifestyle.

We continued deeper into our lifestyle, and I fully embraced it. Things became more complex. New friendships were made, and experiences were had. So many life experiences happened during these years. I took care of a parent, my stepfather passed from cancer.

I became a mother. It was unbelievable and so different from what I had always worried it would be. It took me a long time to decide to be ready and take that leap. I was worried about the genes, worried about finances, and frankly, I could hardly believe I was taking care of myself, much less having the capacity to be responsible for another human being. I was worried I would do it and despise every minute, just as my mother had seemed to experience.

I remember hiring a doula and telling her that I was certain I would experience postpartum depression, so I was preparing and setting up everything to be able to manage through and ensure the baby was well taken care of. I remember telling my doctor the same thing, quoting the statistics and discussing what we should all be on the lookout for post-birth. I remember the slight look of confusion from them as I discussed the topic with such clarity and openness. What I actually experienced ended up being very different.

I loved the feeling of growing a life and how natural and connected it all felt. I remember thinking the clichés are true. Pure love and joy. Excitement and nervousness about the future. The pull I felt to learn and be as a mother as I could be. The fear and panic when something went wrong. Lying in bed rest, praying that the baby was going to be okay. That was the first time I felt my mama bear part—the visceral and instinctive protectiveness, love, and concern of a mother for her child. It all surprised me so much. I truly hadn't thought I would be capable.

Parenting is hard, too, and there were difficult times. Sacrifices were made. I continued to travel for work. We had a lot of help, but it was still very hard on my husband. He picked up a lot of work to care for and maintain the family. And frankly, it was probably too much. He was not one of those guys who abstained from household or parenting responsibilities while creating chaos in other ways. He was very actively involved. His service, along with the nannies, allowed me to continue my career and spend more quality time with my boys, loving on them when I was home. I am certain there are many things I could have done better.

I had some ups and downs in my career, but in general, more ups than downs as things continued to progress. I grew and advanced in my leadership roles. I wanted to feel safe and secure. I wanted to be loved and adored. I wanted to be in a beautiful home. I wanted to be an amazing parent.

In many ways, the relationship structure fed those needs and enabled some of it to work. And for a while, it did work, brilliantly. I was kicking ass at the job, spending time with the baby, making organic homemade baby food, pumping and breastfeeding, playing the part, and letting loose my wild side behind closed doors. The perfect balance and setup. And the perfect cover-up for something that could become more sinister.

In those alternative relationships where you have one person in a leadership role, there is a responsibility and burden that comes along with it. These relationships are not one-dimensional, and there are many aspects to consider related to psychological safety, communication, empowerment, discovery, and acceptance. As part of that process, you are learning each other's limits, boundaries, and needs. There is trust, a dynamic, and an exchange. If you're leading someone, just like in the business world, they are putting trust and faith in you. And you, as a leader, have the responsibility to make good decisions in that person's best interest for the right reasons, guiding them in the right way. This is where things can get twisted, lines in life can get blurred, and toxic co-dependencies can develop. All of which they did. There were incredible highs, and the lows came crashing in like a tsunami.

In our intimate relationship dynamic, I never performed well enough, never wanted it enough, never did enough, never could meet the need, no matter what. And I was alone. Who do you share the most intimate details of your marriage and life with? Friends? Vanilla people didn't understand this world. People in the same types of relationships? Maybe, but how do I admit what is really going on? I don't know myself. I don't want to burst the bubble in my own mind, much less admit that to someone else. How can I explain to someone that I was pushed to do something and felt guilty about doing it? The pressure I felt. The inner conflict of enjoying things I didn't want to do, or maybe I did? At a certain point, I couldn't tell the difference. Significant boundary violations would happen, tapping into that feeling I knew so well in my being. But it was such a confusing world at times.

Then, the gaslighting. I couldn't see it at the time, but oh god can I see it now. Brilliantly delivered, I learned how to gaslight myself into agreement.

This created an inner battle between holding onto the facade, the dream, the highs of what was going on, versus the reality and my inner voice pushing back. One part, *This is amazing,* while another part is like, *What the fuck? This is awful; this is not you.* One part was screaming inside, while another part was soothed by the needs that were being met.

I saw my own toxicity show up in situations, and I would shame myself. Every situation feeding that cognition of being defective and a bad human being. Anxiety continued to increase. I continued treatment for it. I pushed through. I lived a multi-layered existence as I always had known to do.

Looking back, I can see it's complicated. I see the high that comes when somebody is looking up at you with adoration in their eyes and offering themselves to you. It makes you feel like a powerful goddess. Of course, what actually is happening is that rush of chemicals in the brain and the cycle at play. The same familiar dispensation of oxytocin and dopamine, pathways to follow, things to do, dynamics to play out.

Phase 2b: Reflection and Journaling

"Those Who Do Not Learn History Are Doomed To Repeat It."
- George Santayana

These are wise words. Coping doesn't solve the problem, distance doesn't solve the problem, and time does not heal, not when it comes to trauma. The cycles that manifest themselves here are common among survivors. There is a time to focus on coping and getting through to a place where you can do the work. But if you don't do the work, it will inevitably happen again.

Journal Exercise

- When you consider this example, what cycles were repeating themselves?

  _____

  _____

  _____

  _____

- What repeating cycles can you identify in your own life?

  _____

  _____

  _____

  _____

- What core traumas might they be related to?

  _____

  _____

  _____

  _____

PHASE 3

AWAKENING

CHAPTER 8

RYAN'S CANCER

My brother Ryan died at the age of 36. Going through portions of that fight by his side was a turning point that marked the beginning of my awakening period. Part of that awakening period included getting angry and resentful as I processed through. Part of that journey I excelled at; part of that journey I stumbled horribly. It's all part of the journey.

Ryan was happier than I realized and had more friendships than I knew. He had an artistic side that he was able to express through a local theater group. After years of career struggle, he found his way and finally found a company he enjoyed, and that seemed to enjoy him. He did not know how to experience love: he didn't know what that was, what it looked like, and certainly not what it felt like. Everything for him always came with a price.

I remember thinking to myself that when you are young and sick like he was, you are experiencing simultaneous traumas and loss: the trauma of your body betraying you and dying, and also the trauma of losing the life you'll never live. The love you'll never experience. The kids you'll never hold. The possibility that is lost. It's that possibility that leads to hope, and hope that leads to the yearning of the human experience and the journey we all take. What happens when that hope is gone? Taken by a disease. What happens when we are alone, truly alone, sick and dying? Who is there with us, holding our hand as we walk that journey?

I remember talking to my mother, telling her that she could not complain about boarding the dogs, her boyfriend's knee surgery, or whatever the fuck she found to complain about (always a price). "Your son is dying," I remember saying to her. "If I call you and say you need to come now, you'll fucking come now." Pure toxic.

I can remember her sigh, moan, and groan, and she still complained to him anyway. I'm sorry, Mom, your 36-year-old son is infested with tumors, dying; the last-ditch effort failed, and we are about to make another Hail Mary at MD Anderson. I'm sorry, though, you'll have to pay to board your dogs to come be by his side!

I realize now that was likely the final conversation she had with him: complaining about boarding her dogs to come visit. An important discovery for me post-mortem. A clarifying moment as a mother and human being. In the final dying days of my young, 36-year-old, single, devastated brother, when he was coming to terms with the reality that his time on this earth was about to end, accepting that he would never feel the romantic love of a woman, be filled with the joy, light, and giggle of his child's laughter, or know the true peace of self-acceptance. In those final days, my dutiful, committed, caring, attentive mother was completely aware of what was happening and acutely aware of what it's like for someone to face that final death journey from her own cancer experience with my stepfather with tumors that had invaded his body like a roach infestation, expanding before liquefying the organs they ate away. Ryan was at the moment with no turning back. Knowing all those things, what did she do? I can't tell you. I don't know what she did. But I know what she didn't do. She did not text, did not call, did not email, did not relay a message through me to him, did not get on a plane for six days until he was about to die in the ICU. Nothing. Silence. Absence. No "I love you." No "I'll be there for you." No "I'm sorry this is happening to you." No nothing. That was clarifying.

It was MLK Jr. weekend. On the last day of his life, I called and told her to come immediately, and she did. They all did, then. Of course. Gotta at least be there for that so you can say you were there, right? Except during his last moments, she was also complaining, this time about his music playing in the background. If it's not one thing, it's another. And it is always about her. Ryan always had a tremendous love of music, certain bands, and certain songs. Two of them were the Beatles and U2. He also had a love of U.S. history, had studied it in college, taught it in schools, and traveled the world to see it.

The things they don't know until you've gone through it are the realities of the biological processes at play, as the body is overcome by the toxicity of the cancer infestation, and systems and organs are shutting down. But it doesn't happen immediately upon making the decision not to intervene. It's hard. He was scared. I could feel it. Luckily, I knew his phone password and put on some of his music in the background. In response, a certain someone in the room crinkled her nose and said, "Do we have to listen to this?" with a complaining tone. I remember having a glimpse of surprise at the comment, but it was fleeting: of course, this was her response! I said, "Yes, we do. It's Ryan's music that will be comforting to him. He needs some help with this last part."

"Hey Jude" by the Beatles finishes, and I hear the music start. U2's "MLK." The final moments are here. We can feel it. I can see it in his eyes. He is scared. He doesn't want to let go. He knows it's happening. He is sad. **I'm so so so sorry. I'm so sorry I couldn't protect you. I'm so sorry I couldn't fix this. I am so sorry we are here. You do not deserve this. You didn't deserve any of this. I'm sorry. Please don't go. Please, please, please don't go.**

Bono's voice starts. . .

> *Sleep*
> *Sleep tonight*
> *And may your dreams*
> *Be realized*
> *If the thundercloud*
> *Passes rain*
> *So let it rain*
> *Rain down on him*
> *Mmm*
> *So let it be*
> *Mmm*
> *So let it be*
> *Sleep*
> *Sleep tonight*
> *And may your dreams*
> *Be realized*
> *If the thundercloud*
> *Passes rain*
> *So let it rain*
> *Let it rain*
> *Rain on him*

(Source: LyricFind)

And then he was gone forever.

Ryan deserved so much better. Underneath a sometimes grisly exterior, he was kind, sensitive, gentle, intelligent, funny, and loving. He was a good soul who cared about humanity, saw the world through a teacher's eyes, tried to help others, and desperately wanted to be loved. That gnawing, aching pain never left him. That bottomless pit of self-loathing never filled. Long before cancer and into early diagnosis, he battled deep depression and, many times, did not want to live. We would joke about not carrying on the defective genes to a new generation and ending the mutation with us.

We fought like brothers and sisters did, including fights I'll always deeply regret. Things I wish I could take back. Things I wish I would have done better. *More compassion* I wish I would have shown. *More kind and present* I wish I had been.

Let's go back to earlier in the story...

After the initial C scare and fight, we thought he had made it. The surgery was a success. The immunotherapy worked. All was clear. On the mend. It just didn't stay that way for long. Shortly after his 35th birthday, the melanoma was back, had metastasized, and we geared up for battle.

It included more surgery, more intensive chemo, more radiation, more immunotherapy, more of anything and everything we could do to slow it down and buy time. My sister and I tried to support him. My mother contributed too, on her terms, in her way, with her pain, always at a cost. We scoured the earth for solutions, talked to every connection we had, and made our way through the best cancer treatment hospitals in the country. Sometimes, the best thing I could do for him was get the weed. By the time we got to the NIH, Sarah, my ex, and I rotated days in Bethesda to be by his side during a five-week clinical trial. They had taken some pity on him and advocated to get him into the trial, even though by this time, it was up his spine, on his lungs, in his brain. He was barely eating and was often being admitted to the hospital due to weakness and side effects. Brutal is the word.

*After the five-week NIH treatment, somehow, I convinced him to spend his birthday and Christmas with me in Dallas and told him that we would go together back to the NIH for the follow-up. He could barely eat a spoonful of food by this time. It's surprising he was still alive. Three weeks later, as I walked down the halls of the NIH Cancer Institute, I could hear the bloodcurdling, haunting screams of children in pain echoing down the corridors. My heart broke. It bled. And I sank to the floor. **Please, please, please don't let him die. Please, this cannot be it. This cannot be his story. This cannot be his life. This cannot be happening.***

The nurses and doctors were crying as they told us the news on NYE 2015. There was no hope. It had spread everywhere, and they couldn't fight it back. They couldn't slow it down. In fact, it was speeding up, getting more and more aggressive, hungrier, and hungrier as it ravaged and consumed the insides of his body like a horror film. He was going to die.

Two days later, we were on a flight back to Dallas, scheduling doctors and a trip to MD Anderson. We refused to accept that Ryan was going to die.

The next three weeks were a blur of doctor's appointments, palliative care, getting his cat Delilah down to Dallas, and planning the trip to MD Anderson. Ryan was not going to give up. We talked about his wishes if it were to happen, including the very clear directions not to allow our father to "pretend to be a great dad" at his funeral, "talking or saying anything" during any kind of memorial. He was crystal clear that he did not want his life and death to become fodder for further exploitation. But to be clear, to him, death was still far from an accepted outcome. At one point, he even considered going back to work.

The nannies, my then-husband, my son, and everyone else wrapped around him as we gave him palliative care those weeks—doctor's visits, medication routines, trying to keep his body functioning. Everyone pitched in.

Then it was time to make the trip back to MD Anderson to see if it had worked. He was in delirium the whole way down to Houston from Dallas, hallucinating that nurses were behind us, puking into every bag I desperately

found, having come completely ill-prepared—the car filled with the acidic reek
of vomit. Four hours later, we were in the doctor's office for a consultation. They
looked at me, puzzled. I could hear them saying with their eyes, "You don't seem
to understand what is happening here; he is about to die." He was admitted. Six
days later, he was gone forever.

I think a lot about the lessons that Ryan taught me. In our last lucid,
complete conversation, after the MD Anderson doctor told him he had days to
live and suggested he sign a non-resuscitation order, we took a walk (me pushing
his wheelchair) to the atrium of the hospital. After strolling around a little, we
settled in an area filled with plants and light and talked. I asked him if he
wanted to sign the order. He looked at me and laughed. Then he said, "Fuck this
place, let's go to Cancer Centers of America." And he was dead serious.

So our last bits of conversation (there were small moments of lucidity) were
about planning a momentous road trip—in an RV with his cat, a nurse, and
lots of weed. Planning to go from Dallas to the Grand Canyon, to Joshua Tree,
and then to Cancer Centers of America. We had some good laughs thinking and
planning that out over the weekend. That was before he slipped into total
delirium, and we never spoke again. I'm still planning to take him there.

The lesson he taught me in that last stand, in that determination from a
kid who for much of his life did not want to live, was the courage to fight for
your life. The fundamental importance of your child experiencing your love.
Love is indeed an action. The gift of laughter, being kind and present. The
capacity that I actually do have to give love and care. I will always and forever
be grateful to him for giving me those gifts and for his fierce determination to
fight to the very end.

The final gift Ryan gave me in his death was the courage to love myself
enough to break free from two people who always did, and always would,
cause hurt and damage. I don't want to share the awful things that happened
in the months following his death, the final straws, the final interactions that
closed those relationships from harming forevermore. I am no innocent

angel, either. I've done the work, purged the toxicity out, and let go of it all. They will never, ever hurt my children via their presence or their absence. I broke the shackles off one hand. Now it was time to break them off the other.

CHAPTER 9

TOXICITY STRENGTHENS ITS GRIP

I realized how important it was that my son not live his life as an only child and how important sibling relationships were. I didn't ever want him to be alone after we were gone and facing things that Ryan faced. So we decided to have another child. I got pregnant fairly quickly and had my second child. While this was happening, my career continued to advance, and I got more senior leadership roles. This also puts stress on the marriage with each one of those steps, probably for a lot of reasons, including the stress that everybody faces with young kids, households, travel, and just the energy to keep the wheel moving. I also started to become more aware of the constant energy drain and deficit that I felt and that inner voice screaming louder and louder that something was wrong. I just couldn't keep up.

Our social life and image at this point was this perfect, beautiful family: professional couple, gorgeous home, wonderful kids, sexy life. People sought us out as mentors. It was all very postcard-worthy.

The structure of it all became complicated and taxing. It's confusing. Some things I felt pressured into doing that I did not naturally want to do. But some of it I did, and I certainly found things I enjoyed. Regardless, it wasn't a healthy dynamic, and there was a toxic undercurrent to it all.

There was always a price to pay. Typically because I was doing the thing, but I wasn't; either I enjoyed it too much, or I enjoyed it too little, or I didn't pay enough attention, or I paid too much attention, or whatever the fuck it was. I could never do it right, and I was never good enough.

Things started to turn glaringly toxic. Boundaries were violated. Volatile cycles and blow-ups happened before big or important events. My career continued to bring pressure to the marriage, more demand on the team that operated the mechanics of our life, and more pressure and drain on energy and resources. Living the dream while paying the price.

It became clear that my second child had some special needs. In those early months, I started to identify it, and we began talking about it with his caregivers and each other. Of course, I internalized those gaps as a deficit in some part of mine, which became leverage that was used later when I broke. "I must not be attentive enough," "I am working too much," "I was too old when I had him." But I had these amazing caregivers with me, loving on him 24/7, and a husband who worked very hard at caregiving through those months, too, picking up more than half of his labor with my work travel and our complicated life. It was a conscious decision we made together, but nonetheless hard to execute, with a lot of sacrifices all the way around.

It was a lot to contend with and reminded me of running shifts in restaurants from my early years. Parents of young kids are often exhausted. When one parent is traveling, combined with all this other stuff, it adds stress to the unit, and all other members pick up more. When balls are dropped, or the system goes offline for any number of variable reasons, it's painful, and all stakeholders are failed. My ambition was fueled by that fundamental crack; the need to continue to achieve on all fronts certainly created its own level of pressure. My ambition included parenting, always looking for ways to make things better, work better, ensure the boys have a good life, feel loved, and have a secure attachment style, healthy bodies and minds. More important than my own insecurities was the actual outcome of those important goals and priorities related to their development, while equally petrified of destroying them through my own ineptitude.

Up until then, I'd had a great relationship with my in-laws. I thought they had a perfect family, the family I had never experienced and so longed to achieve. I deeply respected their journey and their story of coming to America, with all their trials and tribulations. I idolized and romanticized them. I thought we were close. They had helped me plan my wedding, and we spent vacations together. They were getting older and lived out in Northern California, and with our kids being young, it was difficult to visit. It takes a lot—flights and a drive while hauling two little kids isn't the easiest trip, especially with a busy and draining career in the balance. They started to have some health issues. I had a brilliant idea about them moving to Texas to be near us and the kids. I wanted the boys to have family around them. To experience what I didn't. And so they did.

Something shifted when they came. We were no longer enjoying each other's company on holiday; we were in more formal roles. They wanted to assume these more traditional patriarch and matriarch roles of the family and for me to submit to their direction. I hadn't experienced that type of dominance since early on in my life.

They were at the house all the time, constantly watching, criticizing, evaluating. I could see them, feel the judgment, the confusion, the negativity. Scrutinizing every detail of our lives, all the time.

What felt sudden and strange was their struggle with me on things that were not new. Comments about my travel and disapproval of nannies, which is interesting given they had multiple nannies in South America with their young kids. I'm not a hands-off mother. I was very engaged with the kids. I just also believe that more love and care is better than less. And I knew how taxing careers and travel were, so I set up a system and built a village for the long term. We are all raising them together in our respective roles. The approach worked brilliantly, and I believe it's a key reason the boys are so resilient and happy today.

At first, I was confused by my in-laws' judgment and reaction to me. She had worked when they were growing up. She was well-educated and did not have to be beholden to a man. Then I realized she did work and took care of the kids. There were major life transitions they went through when the boys were young that had an impact on all of them. The work wasn't a career; it was punching a clock. The roles at home were very traditional, with the labor falling on her on top of a full-time job. That was in stark contrast to our life. I was in a business leadership role, and, if anything, the household roles were reversed, mainly by encouragement, the arithmetic of income trajectory, and impact on our overall portfolio, personal preferences, and the conscious choices we made together. But the guilt and judgment that came infected.

They just couldn't understand it. And I remember my father-in-law once looking at me and saying, "I just don't understand you. You have people who do things for you." And I looked at him and said, "You mean you don't understand an executive woman?" By this point, I'm starting to feel antagonistic as I react to the scrutiny and disapproval. I'm 12 again in church. Yes, I have somebody who works in the garden. I have somebody who cleans the house. I have people who help with the kids, all those things. So I can spend quality time with them and your son when I'm in town. We recognize the privilege we have in being able to build this life.

I want to say, "By the way, your son's got me doing all this crazy fucking shit that's keeping me up half the night, that's got me completely fucking drained of every ounce of energy." I hold that back and just try to understand how they could be reacting and attempt to put their minds at ease. I was foolish and arrogant to think I could pull that off.

Ultimately, they accused me of things that were devastating to be accused of. Gloria Dei. They didn't stop. They continued with an intrusive, persistent, almost investigative lens into our lives, making things very uncomfortable. He buckled under the pressure and told his parents selective truths that portrayed an image that was not fully accurate and very damaging to me. Kaboom.

The relationships were completely destroyed. They hated me and were so angry that we brought them to Texas. They should have never come, and I've shattered their dreams. I'm an awful human being. I am a worthless whore. I'm 17 again. Discard.

There is torment, and things are spinning out of control. After my usual nightly cocktail of Ambien to knock myself into sleep, in the middle of the night, I wake up suddenly to events leaving me feeling deeply violated and in panic. I'm in pigtails again.

Spiraling fast. I have this huge chasm in my marriage and a sense of betrayal felt by all. The false pretense of our life crumbles. I am exhausted, completely depleted, on every level possible.

I remember thinking at one point that maybe I'm just this person who doesn't have that much energy because all I want to do is sleep. I daydream about rest. Keep in mind, I'm leading HR, I'm traveling the country, we've got two young kids, I'm managing the household, life, and all this relationship torment.

Overload. I so desperately wanted to hold on to it; I wanted to make it work. I can't stop seeing some patterns more clearly now. Not knowing what I'm starting to realize, I just know that this is now toxic and unhealthy. No one is in a good place. Screaming on the inside.

I was petrified of becoming my mother. That was a constant narrative. I was petrified of fucking up my life. Toxic people know your vulnerabilities and instinctively and ruthlessly use them to control you. Part of understanding the cycle is looking at the darkest things within you, the secrets you keep, the shame that clouds your soul, and shining a light on it. Recognize the parts of ourselves that are toxic, our own contributions to scenarios, and take accountability for those contributions while also recognizing the complicated truths and conditioning that fueled them. This is not simple to do.

Shame grips your soul and squeezes the air from your lungs. Coercive control and sexual exploitation are very common in survivor stories. It's not unusual for dysfunctional and destructive behaviors to occur as a result. Go to any AA/NA group, and you'll find survivors. The nature of this particular type of exploitation makes it very difficult to talk about, which is precisely why

I am doing so. This is why I share this in context with my career story—to hold a light up and say, "You can do this; it's okay to be a human being." It is not a new lesson that material success does not equal perfectionism or some unrealistic idea and standard of who people actually are.

So many survivors experience situations where they were pushed, pressured, and ultimately coerced to do things that they hold guilt and shame for. It's a damaging twisting of sexuality and of things that, in a healthy relationship, can be beautiful and amazing. They are not the same thing. And because of the nature of our tendency to shame for sexuality, sexual preferences, or interests, toxic situations can be more easily hidden and more easily isolating. Who are you going to talk to about it? You don't even want to talk to yourself, much less face the shock and shame from someone else. Even those in the world you are in don't understand what is actually happening. Bursting your fantasy bubble means bursting theirs too.

CHAPTER 10

2020

Running. Running up a steep hill. Heart pounding, breath rasping, petrified, faster and faster. Sweat dripping down my face as the hot sun penetrates. Pushing my legs down to take the next big step, pushing harder and harder as fast as I can possibly go. Away from what is chasing at my back, I'm barely out of its grasp. Running to... something. Running to a dream. I'm at the top, still in a nightmare.

In the fall of 2019, I got offered a job. It was a big promotion, and in South Florida, between Miami and Fort Lauderdale. I took it. We talked it over together. We were struggling in the marriage. At that point, still trying to find our way back, we'd started marriage therapy and counseling. I am not a perfect participant. I'm also going to individual therapy with an incredible therapist for whom I will always be deeply grateful.

Therapy and starting to actively own and treat what was happening was, for me, an important aspect of the first HiveStrong step: **Put your own oxygen mask on first**. At this point in the journey, your brain is foggy, your energy is running on deficit, you are emotionally spent, your confidence is zero, and you probably have some bad coping behaviors. You are feeling more and more cognitive dissonance with what is happening around you, questioning all of your thoughts, realities, beliefs, and truths. You are pulling on internal reserves to keep the balls of life rolling. Your world is crumbling. You look in the mirror, and it explodes into a million pieces, leaving a bloody, cut distortion of the person you once were. This is a painful time in the awakening phase. This is where you are breaking down further and further.

You have to put the oxygen mask on yourself first for a very scientific reason. It is not "wooey psychobabble." When the lizard brain is in control, to ultimately navigate through these circumstances successfully, the number one priority is bringing ourselves back to baseline, mentally and physically. That is what allows the limbic system to calm, and executive functioning to come back online. Understanding the science of what trauma and triggers do to our brain, allows us to intentionally act on that neuroscience to make better decisions and improve overall outcomes.

Increasing and repeating self-care and compassion is essential to giving yourself the inner strength you will need. What that looks like is unique to each of us as individuals. That said, it is strongly recommended to get the right, trauma-informed therapist who is adept at multiple modalities and has a toolkit to customize and address that trauma. Put oxygen into your lungs and breathe.

Learn more about how the brain functions during trauma and how to leverage that insight to manage it more effectively.
SCAN THE QR CODE:

South Florida ends up being a great opportunity for a while. It enables a mini-separation as I'm in Fort Lauderdale for ten days a month (every other work week). I arrange an agreement where, instead of moving the family right away, we get to the end of the school year in 2020 and then move the clan. So this becomes the plan we make together. I also want to take a moment to

acknowledge how hard it had to have been to be a parent at home with young kids. Even with the help, it's still hard. I know that. I think women have been doing this for decades. It is still unusual for a man to assume that role.

I'm exhausted, transitioning to a new gig, high intensity. Because I have a break from the environment for a few days at a time, I start to see the pattern. I start to notice and observe some of the differences in my own body. And I'm starting to do the work with my therapist as well around my own anxiety and issues. At this point, I can feel the anxiety in my body, I can feel it in my energy, and I can feel, in some ways, my energy increase when I'm away from the environment at home. But it also showed up in some really negative ways. I could almost feel and see the ripple effect. I could feel the toxicity. As mentioned in earlier chapters, part of the shame that keeps you trapped is not being an "innocent victim." You're in a toxic situation. It poisons you. That toxicity poisons your body, your mind, and your energy, and it affects every part of you. It's not compartmentalized to just one aspect of your life. It shows up in all of them, as my experience demonstrates clearly.

I have a picture from the holidays where I have deep bags and dark circles under my eyes, and the look on my face is one of complete depletion. I tell Liz, my therapist, I'm ready to do Eye Movement Desensitization and Reprocessing (EMDR). We have been talking about it for a year by this point; I just hadn't been ready to pull the trigger. I have to do something because I'm constantly feeling like a bad mom and a horrible human being.

Do the Work, Then Do It Again

We set up our first EMDR intensive week to address that "bad mom" target, including her tentacles of triggers. EMDR intensives are one hour a day for four to five days of EMDR. An EMDR intensive for a week is very hard work, incredibly cathartic, and for me, highly effective. It doesn't completely take away the sensitivity or fear (not quite Eternal Sunshine of the Spotless Mind*). I mean, what mother isn't worried about being a bad mom? If you aren't worried about being a bad mom, stop and talk to your doctor.*

Moms should care, and none of us are perfect. But there's a difference between recognizing that you're not perfect, wanting to raise your kids well, and continuing to examine, adjust, learn, and grow. That's healthy. But what's not healthy is being paralyzed and consumed and being told and made to feel that you're a piece of shit, you're horrible, and you're totally fucking up your kids for life. That is paralyzing, activates the lizard brain, and leads to very poor outcomes.

I liken EMDR to mental surgery. When the trauma happens, it creates a neural pathway that I often refer to as "trauma wiring." That wiring doesn't go away or lessen in strength over time. In toxic relationships, this is the wiring that is created, existing lines tapped into, and used to facilitate your self-destruction in a manner that continues the psychological control that the other person has over you. You have to grab it and rip it all up and wire yourself in a healthy way around that topic.

The intensive helped me to rewire that cognition and release its grip on me. Instead of being a bad mom who's absent, a horrible fuck-up, abandoning her family, and fucking up her kids, I am a good mom. I'm a dedicated mom, deeply concerned with ensuring my children have an amazing life and childhood filled with love, care, and wonderful people supporting them. I'm a good mom who loves her kids and provides for their futures. Not perfect. Perfection isn't the goal. Happy, healthy kids are the true North.

This is a critical action that leads to a power shift in a toxic relationship and a step forward in turning your pain into power. When you rip up those lines, there isn't the same infrastructure for someone to tap into and exploit to their advantage. They can't get you destabilized by it. They can't use that destabilization to create chaos and more shame. They simply can't touch you. And all of a sudden, you are the one in control of yourself and the destiny of your family.

I've done years and years of talk therapy to this point (which I still think is really important to do in conjunction). But holy fucking shit, that one week of four EMDR sessions saved my life… rapidly. No longer in constant panic and lizard brain from being triggered on this topic, I was calmer, and my executive functioning, more operational. That enabled me to see the pattern of what was at play and navigate through it without going through such exhausting highs and lows on a roller-coaster through it. I felt the shift in the relationship cycle, almost in disbelief. And now that I could see it, I was getting stronger and closer to the mindset it would take to break free. It is important to note that I did not call it abuse at this time. I didn't believe I was being abused. I simply thought, This situation is not healthy, and this marriage may not last.

January 2020

My two childhood friends since kindergarten come to visit me for a weekend in Fort Lauderdale, staying at my apartment. One of my girlfriends tells me all about her horrific divorce from her narcissistic, abusive husband, which is currently in its third year. I learn so much by just listening and hearing her story. So much registers in my brain that I don't even realize, but later it will come up. Mostly, I was just being an empathetic friend, holding a safe space, supporting. Lots of hanging by the pool; she was understandably too exhausted for outside shenanigans. I remember her walking through the door, now in a safe space, collapsing from exhaustion.

March 2020

The pandemic hits. I am spending half my time in Florida at this point, leading a national restaurant company that saw revenue decline by ~80% in three days (a story for another time). We are private equity-held, and we are going to have to bare-knuckle through it. It takes a tremendous amount of energy, focus, and leadership. People are scared, devastated, destabilized. Three thousand employees whose lives had just been turned upside down needed help to navigate through what became a period of ongoing, collective, community trauma.

On one side, I'm bringing trauma-informed leadership, channeling my own care and learning to this business situation I'm in the middle of, and on the other side, I am going through a period of rapid awakening and massive personal devastation while trying to make sure the boys stay protected, healthy, and educated through it all. I don't want to let go. I don't want to give up on the marriage but increasingly see that this just isn't healthy. I am consumed by guilt and shame for even thinking about divorce.

I channel the pain and energy into supporting and leading people through crises in the role I am in. It's one of the superpowers you have as a trauma survivor. We are people who know how to navigate craziness. The ones who are familiar with that space. The people you want in that foxhole. There is resilience.

I'm in hero mode at work, and the cycle continues at home. Finally, at 2:00 a.m. on Mother's Day, I say the words: "I want a divorce." I'm not surprised by the response. **You'll never find anyone who loves you like I love you. You'll never have anyone do what I do. You are going to fuck up the boys just like you got fucked up. You are a fuck up. You're devastating me. I'm the one who has created this life for you. I'm the reason you have stability. I'm the reason you have money. And you're going to fuck it all up.** *I believe, with every cell of my being, that he is right.*

Those statements were untrue then, untrue later, and are untrue today. Why would I believe such horrible things with so much evidence to the contrary? I call this out because it is a powerful part of the cycle that often keeps victims trapped. There is a difference between knowing something intellectually from facts and what you *feel* is *true*. This cognitive dissonance is confusing for the victim and often keeps them trapped.

What I also learned later is that these are very common strategies used in all sorts of toxic situations to maintain power.

"You will never find anybody who loves you as much as I love you. I'm the only one who will accept you as you are. No one will do these things for you. You are going to fuck up your entire life and everyone around you by making this decision."

In reality, I was dying, and I was doing the only thing I could do to stop it. I knew I was going down that old, familiar deep, dark hole. But this time, I couldn't. There was a voice inside me that said, You have to do this to survive. And at that point, survive, is all I could do.

CHAPTER 11

BREAKING FREE

I've said the words. They hang in the air. I feel bad for being the one to say them. I am the villain, for sure. I'm trying to be kind. I've destroyed the dream.

For some reason, I think I'm going to be able to do this amicably. I'm even considering a cohabitating scenario. It's ridiculous to think that was actually going to be possible. Leading through the pandemic and all the stuff that's going on, I'm still coming back and forth between Dallas and Florida. Even though it's a pandemic, I still fly, as I just need the space, and the tickets are dirt cheap. I need a break. I have to hold it together.

I do my job, and I do it really well. The unique circumstances and channeling allow me to lead in a special and highly effective way, which, combined with the collective leadership of the team and a fantastic PR partner, leads to remarkable results, press, awards, blah blah. Not the purpose of this story.

As things proceed with the divorce, I start having certain experiences and realizations. Control over the money, access to it, and transparency become central issues. This was supposed to be simple and straightforward, but it's not. And now the intel that my friend has given me from sharing her story on that girls' weekend in January really starts to come into play. I see the parallels. I can start to anticipate the moves. Which also means there is another truth I have yet to come to terms with.

June 2020

Laid out on the bed, gazing out the window to the garden I once labored in for hours. My arms and legs were bruised, my leg propped up to help the ankle swelling. My mind swimming in torment and spinning, and I start to float away. First up above my body, floating to the ceiling, looking down in shock and disbelief. Not sure if I'm dreaming, having a nightmare, or watching a movie. Holy fucking shit, who am I? How did I get here? Is this real?

I turn my head toward the television and see the country exploding. George Floyd. Murder. Eight minutes. Horror. Played over and over. The world is on fire inside and out. There is a sickness, torment, and despair that comes from knowing that you are powerless against the evil that is destroying you.

I replay events over and over again. It's my fault. I'm embarrassed. I'm to blame. I'm wrong.

It's a strange experience when the dissociation starts. It's a combination of numbing, distance, and floating. It's a different world within the same world, except you aren't really part of either one. Maybe I should just disappear, change my name, move to some tiny existence in a faraway town, keep my head down, not say a word to anyone, and disappear on my own.

Become the nothing that I am.

This thought rolls around and around in my head, and I start to visualize this alternative life.

Away from causing and receiving constant pain and never-ending need. Away from everyone and everything. An existence of numbness. Except I know that numbness isn't enough. It's really black nothingness that is needed. The thought is appealing. It's not the first time.

I'm hanging on a cliff's edge by a fingernail. The calm of that vast, deep, engulfing blackness starts to come over me. It's strong, it's seductive, a pull… a longing… a relief, a place that feels so familiar, like I belong, I've been there before. I'm floating away, calm because now I know the answer, and there is an endpoint to the torment that consumes my being.

I close my eyes and see the boys' smiling faces. Their whole faces light up when they smile. Eyes bright, mouths wide open with the corners turned up, giggles escaping, pure joy and delight. It's the most beautiful sight I've ever seen.

Then I see them as teenagers. I see the pain a child feels when they realize their parent is more consumed by their own pain than by the capacity to love them unconditionally. The pain of believing that love wasn't deserved. The pain of knowing nothing will ever be good enough to fix it or fill the gaping, bleeding hole that is left with your violent absence. Desperate attempts to feed or cover fail miserably time and time again. The ache of longing for the acceptance and comfort that only a parent can give a child and that will never come. The loneliness that happens when one doesn't know how to love or be loved.

Instantly, I know what I have to do. I cannot leave these beautiful boys and condemn them to a lifetime of pain. No fucking way. What the fuck. These sweet, beautiful, special, loving souls deserve better. I don't, but they do. And I have to do it for them, if for nothing else.

Over the course of two days, a series of highly caustic interactions had occurred. At a certain point in the exchange, in an act to amplify the humiliation while hurling insult after insult, he also turns his video recording on and points the camera at my face to capture my reaction and physical response of breaking down completely. It was "Rachael's Insecurities Greatest Hits" played out over and over again, with an air of wicked delight at my undoing. I can remember looking up in pain and confusion, tears streaming down my face, and asking, "Why are you doing this?" **I'm 17 again.**

Mind racing, heart pounding, eyes pouring. **"Why does he want to capture me on video breaking down and crying and screaming? Why does that seem to give him some sickening delight? Is this really happening with the person I trusted my heart and soul to? The only person who really knows me? This is what he thinks? This is what he wants? My utter destruction?"**

This level of hostility continues intermittently for those two days. At one point, I get upset and pick up a copy of the prenup in a moment of drama. I'm upset: I feel he is withholding key information and trying to circumvent the *prenup agreement. The lack of access and transparency to the financial portfolio increases my paranoia. "**He must be hiding something,**" I think to myself. There is no trust. I start to rip it up, in a dramatic act to say it clearly doesn't matter, etc. At a certain point of activation, I can certainly contribute histrionics to the situation, a tendency I dislike.*

He is still recording. He puts the phone down so you can't see what's going on, but you can hear. And what you hear is the sound of him grabbing me by the arms and wrestling with me. You hear my struggle; at some point, my wrists are grabbed as well. You can hear me saying, "Get off me! Get your hands off me! Get off me!" in desperation.

After we struggle for a while, I break free, run to the bedroom, and lock the door. I'm 10 again.

Thirty minutes later, I have a 2.5-hour on-camera executive leadership team meeting. Like every good survivor, I know how to put on the face. I pull it together. I participate very effectively. I cannot miss this. I can't have this kind of bullshit fuck up all these other people and the shit that they're dealing with. I need to be there and deliver. So I do. This also gives a little bit of a break for things to cool down. He doesn't try to interrupt.

Later that night, I'm lying on the bed with my foot propped up due to swelling (somewhere in this series of altercations, I have kicked the wall out of frustration, causing my own pain). I'm icing it and keeping it elevated.

I turn on the news and see mad chaos happening: This is the day that the George Floyd story broke. I'm watching this story about what's happened, and I know shit is about to explode. I know what that means for this country and its people. I know how I'm reacting. I already know how much the pandemic has disproportionately impacted people of color and how much acute pressure and pain those communities are experiencing. It does not take a sociologist to know what is going to happen. It is horrific pain and betrayal played out over and over on our screens. A man dying while begging for his mother and the people in power and control perpetrating it, while others watch helpless and frozen nearby. Horrific. Explosion. Pain. Danger.

The vibe in the house has shifted, and we are now post-explosion. Things have calmed down; it's been a few hours. He is bringing me things, asking if he can bring me anything else. That sheepish, sad person. He doesn't apologize. Instead, he feeds the narrative that has gripped my body, that the altercation is my fault. And that the videos are proof of this. I'm so ashamed. I ask him to delete the videos because I am so ashamed and embarrassed by myself.

He is my caretaker at this point. My mind starts to spin. I start to come outside of my body. I'm floating, watching this whole scene unfold and the craziness on the news, and seeing the two of us interact like we are actors in a movie. Oh my God! Is this really happening? Am I seeing what I think I am seeing?

I think that was probably the moment when the inner warrior part started to stir. She's been there for a long time. It was a watershed moment when I recognized the toxic cycle that was really at play. It hits me like a ton of bricks. Survival mode is on.

Finally, he leaves. Two days later, Richard picks me up, and takes care of me for the next two days before I head back to Florida and face life.

*At this point, I can see the physical marks all over my body: the fingerprints, the handprints, the bruises from the wrestling and struggle. I'm still in shock. I also know I need to focus on the business. The country, and consequently our teams, are in turmoil over the social and racial issues that exploded with George Floyd's murder. Business leaders are not sure how to navigate the situation. They care. They don't want to do the wrong thing. This is before DEI training had taken off. These are difficult and complex issues. It's a difficult line to walk, knowing how to handle that appropriately, compassionately, and professionally—being human to the human beings going through all of this—in a way that helps and doesn't harm. And it's my job to help the team walk this line well. **Do your job, Rachael.***

Radical Acceptance

There is an important step that happens following the initial watershed moment. This step serves as the bridge from "awakening" to success at "breaking free." It's how you translate and move through the shock, awful reality, and truth that you have discovered. It requires you to process the loss of the dream you held onto so tightly for so long—the one you worked and sacrificed for. The dream that was now a nightmare. It is a really hard step to take.

It requires acceptance of the reality of that raw truth, no matter how ugly it is, with open and clear eyes, accepting its reality. Until then, you are fighting it, avoiding it, rationalizing it, hoping you will be wrong. You jump at every clue and twist, hoping it's not the case. How could this be true? In this step, you stop fighting. You stop rationalizing. You stop running away. You see the sharp blade plunged so deeply into your gut, blood pouring out. And you know that you have to pull it out with your bare fucking hands so that you do not die. The trick—what you are *not* doing—is saying that what happened is okay. You STOP gaslighting yourself. It's not okay. It's not your fault. You weren't going to prevent this from happening. I can hold these two thoughts at the same time and handle that cognitive dissonance. And that allows me to pull that knife of torment out and patch up the bleeding hole.

Survivors are desperate to be validated as they learn to hear their own voice and give deference to it. Still petrified of being crazy, stupid, or wrong in some way. Like children learning how to speak, they are often clunky in how that messaging comes out and looks. Sometimes, they can only cry. Their entire world has just been turned upside down, inside out. They need a safe space to know they aren't crazy for calling a spade a spade or thinking these thoughts while still having control over what they decide to do.

I've now worked with people who have acutely horrific and painful truths to accept. Things like:

- I've been trafficked by the person I love and trust.
- My children are being abused and traumatized.

- I've been assaulted and raped.
- The person I love doesn't exist.
- I've been lied to, cheated on, misled.

These are deeply painful truths to come to terms with. Since I've begun to work with survivors through these types of scenarios, I've been struck by how fortunate I was in many ways. And while my experience was different, it was acutely painful. I knew what it really took to take this important step. This was a key moment of the inspiration for me to start HiveStrong.

Radical acceptance is also an important step to transition from a powerless victim to a powerful survivor. Transition the pain and exhaustion of carrying the burden of all of this into fuel and energy that ignites your purpose. Once you let go of the torment of being stuck in that victim loop and the horror of it, you, in turn, get your precious energy back. Fuel. No longer spent on that emotional roller-coaster, you are also no longer distracted and derailed by it. You can see things clearly and calmly. You are getting closer to a clinical and strategic mindset.

I hire my attorney and start to go. At this point, I also know I can't be at home in Texas. The abuse will repeat itself, and that cannot happen. I know exactly where that escalation goes. I find temporary accommodation. I am focused on the boys and ensuring they are getting the educational, physical, and emotional attention they need to get through this so that we don't irrevocably harm them. They are my true north.

I start to read a book called "Becoming the Narcissist's Nightmare" by Shahida Arabi. I vigorously work on myself, keeping the oxygen mask on. I'm having a huge awakening because I'm really now starting to see and understand the patterns from throughout my life. I get amazing advice from people around me, the universe guiding me to each one.

I learn about narcissists and how they use anything they can for power and control to manipulate your behavior, mindfuck you, and drain your energy. I realize that I can map this pattern; now I understand. This is where I start to get very strategic about how I'm going to navigate the situation.

Bobby Fischer Mindset

That's the next step: clinical, cold, strategy. Ten moves ahead. I get a pit bull attorney and put him in a chokehold as if to say, "I'm ready to go. You want to fucking play? You'd best get ready for what I'm about to unleash on you." It's on. I have recordings of some of the conversations from that time period. It's so hard to fight with someone who has known you for 20 years, knows all your stuff, and uses every piece of that intel to mindfuck and undermine you, tapping those trauma wires laid oh so long ago.

At the time, my body and mind really believed those old cognitions, but my mind was also fighting against them. My true inner self. Ultimately, I learned just how wrong those trauma-wiring cognitions were. It turns out, regarding the financials, I actually did contribute equally, if not more. Huh, interesting. I'm actually not an awful mother for getting other people to help take care of the kids and house. This little village/nanny scenario that I set up is actually great because those women insulated the kids so much from what was happening with their dad and I, and their day-to-day lives remained stable through all these massive life changes. The boys feel secure, happy, loved, healthy, and… thriving. Huh. Maybe I'm not a bad mom. Actually, I'm a good one. Noted.

Build and Strengthen Your Hive

I had built a hive of love and support around the boys. Coco & Juan, Tutti & Roger were lifesavers. Coco and Tutti were the boys' nannies. Juan and Roger, their husbands. It worked so much better than I could have ever known. They raised beautiful, loving children and were helping me to raise mine. They loved and supported me, too, if only at times, because they loved those boys.

I was in the throes of negotiating hard at that point, trying to find a new place to live, buy a house, and start to build it out. I'm running and gunning, working on the final parts, getting this divorce done, and battling through all the shit that happens and the back and forth.

We were a team, working together. This was the time of COVID, so we were homeschooling with a tutor, childcare, their husbands, and they were all making sure we all stayed on our routine, were cared for, had special family time together, ate healthy meals, and a million other ways they showed me and the boys love and care.

I would go to Florida and Gaby and Sonia took care of my apartment, food, laundry. Sonia would even put out the heart shaped pillow I had for the boys on my bed so I would see it when I walked in.

Tutti became "COO" of my life in transition, coordinating everything for a brand new house, working with designers and builders, handling all of the craziness that happens when you are trying to build something, and furnish it from top to bottom. I knew the immense privilege I had in being able to do so. I could never have done it alone.

They are doing things because they are employed and paid to do them. But there is a way someone does it that shows their care, concern, love, and support. I wasn't always the easiest, scattered, going through an emotionally difficult divorce, navigating COVID. But they all treated me with kindness, love and understanding. Showing me and the boys unwavering support. Not only did these women create community and family for the boys, but their families did as well. We were navigating, rebuilding, and planning our new life together. Everyone had a voice, and everyone had a part.

True North

I realized I needed to let go of a lot. I needed to let go of things that he thought were important to me so that I could get what I really wanted, which was to be free and free fast. It's not about proving something or getting something; who gives a shit about the bed linen? I can rebuild a home, buy new furniture. None of that mattered. The only thing that really mattered was the look on my kids' faces. Getting free and getting healthy as fast as possible to ensure they have a healthy and happy life. I can rebuild, I can't get back time, more importantly energy, lost fighting over stuff.

Once you've actually let go of the "stuff" that was once important to you, it becomes a powerful tool in your arsenal. Leverage. And I used it. I advocated intelligently and with determination, but fairly. Love your kids more than anything else. Total destruction of the other person does not lead to successful outcomes for the kids, or yourself. Don't act on revenge. Only use the power for good. Stay grounded in your core values. It's an important line to walk. At the inevitable final stand, double down and be strong.

I didn't expect what was coming next and would learn the real importance of these lessons.

Sudden Death

Gone.

Richard was my best friend. He supported me through the roller coaster of these years. Helped me care for the kids, the house, the garden, my wardrobe, sometimes even my coffee. As a recovering alcoholic, he was focused on his own journey, staying on track with the 12 steps, giving back to others. He was my confidant, my cheerleader, my defender. Sometimes too much so. He was the first and last text of the day. Helped me through all the heavy lifting that happens moving around in temp living. He listened to me for endless hours processing. He took care of me while I was healing from wounds. And then, he was gone.

There is a deep ache in longing to experience the joy and amazement of perseverance with someone who saw you at your weakest and supported you unconditionally. Richard was that person. He walked me through the darkness and believed in me when I didn't believe in myself. He was my lifeline, gone, without warning, in an instant, forever. Leaving that familiar, gaping hole of bleeding pain and emptiness.

The very moment Richard died, I was wrangling a bunch of balloons from a party store where I'd over-ordered for a baby shower. I woke up feeling jittery, and as the day progressed, the jitteriness never left; in fact, it became worse. It was my job to pick up the balloons and bring them to the host's house. I had ordered something like 15 large bouquets and could maybe fit two in my car if I was lucky. I wasn't lucky. The wind was so strong, and I didn't anticipate the need for the executive thinking and skill required to bring balloons from the store to my car in the parking lot.

I stood outside my car, trying to get these balloons pushed inside enough for me to close my door, but they just would not go in. I tried everything I could to get these fucking balloons inside my car. The longer it went on, the more worked up and upset I became, to the point where I started shaking and crying because I couldn't get them in the car. I became entangled in the balloons whipping around in the wind, trying violently to escape my grasp. The longer it went on, the more tangled I became until I completely lost control and broke down. I started shaking, crying, and wailing, bent over in emotional pain. I was standing next to my soccer mom's SUV in a suburban Party City parking lot. The balloons fought me harder and harder, getting caught in my hair, wrapped around the door handle, flipped over the top of the car, and they just wouldn't go inside it. My tears increased in intensity every second as I couldn't hold on. My heart was pounding, my head was spinning, my soul screaming.

I gave up. I stopped fighting. I sank to the ground. I took a deep breath, letting the balloon ribbons slip from my fingers, and watched them float away into the sky. They weren't meant to stay. Goodbye.

Three lingering balloons managed to make their way into my car. I was such an obvious disaster that a very nice woman and her teenage son came over to help me. They knew the pain I was in wasn't because of the frigging balloons.

I could see the empathy and understanding in their eyes, along with their concern.

After picking myself off the ground, I calmed down, thanked them, and assured them that I was okay. I got into my car and, after a few minutes, started making my way to the shower. On my way, I started to break down again and cry, and I started to text him: "Something is wrong. I think I'm losing my mind." I was such a mess by the time I got there; I simply dropped off the balloons, apologized, and left. I was now in a blur of tears and confusion, trying to convince myself I was just a hot mess and needed to adjust my meds. I was still jittery when I got home. The rest of the afternoon, I texted and texted, but got no response. I told myself he was resting, he was busy, he was doing something.

When the police called that evening, I already knew. Now I was on the floor, screaming, "NOOOOOOOOOOOOOOO!" at the top of my lungs, sobbing and shaking, pounding the floor, face red, tears gushing down my face.

He was gone. He left that afternoon. He told me at that moment: I felt him, I heard him, and I watched him float away. He was gone forever.

I carry him with me. His voice tells me I can do it, reminding me that I'm going to be okay, that I am loved, and that I am not alone. His ring became a commitment ring to myself, and every time I look down at my hands, I am reminded. I close my eyes, and I can hear his voice, feel his hugs around me, and rest my head on his chest. And for a moment, I feel safe again.

I wish I would have pushed him to go to the doctor. I wish I would have paused my own chaos and reminded him one more time how much I cared. I wish I could go back and show compassion in the times I didn't. I wish I wouldn't have pushed him away. I wish a lot had been different.

He is sad and reminds me that he always knew he would die young and that I had to learn that I could do it on my own. He was there, in the flesh, for a time, for a reason. He helped me. I wouldn't have made it otherwise. But the next part I had to do on my own. Standing on my own two feet. Falling on my own ass. Getting back up. Showing myself that I am enough.

Brass Knuckles

The weeks following Richard's death were a turning point in bringing to closure an intense conflict and battering divorce. I was devastated, bleeding, raw, empty, drained. But I wasn't giving in. Instead, I bled and bled and fed on my pain, turning it into my power. Toxic situations are dark and ugly, with no good guys and no winners. The longer they go, the worse they get. And I certainly did not like the side of myself that had come out to fight. The kids are the only thing that matters. The key is getting it done and over as quickly and efficiently as possible. Take the hits, and when ready, hit back hard with brass knuckles on. One and done. That's best for everyone. I refueled myself, got my grip, and punched my way out, this time for good.

In the final break of every toxic cycle, there is a crescendo that happens, a last pounding, a final round, a moment of reckoning. This is the moment in negotiations, after being worn down punch by punch, round after round, where your true survivor strength emerges. You have already walked through hell. You can walk through this.

You've been hit in every way, from every angle, mercilessly, and the other person is coming in for one final punch to take you out for good. In nature, it's where the predator, seeing the weakened enemy scrambling, smelling the blood dripping from her wounds, knowing she's almost ready to die, paces, licks its lips in anticipation, almost there. It is a moment of reckoning, and it is a moment that happens right before the break in every cycle. The predator expects the prey to die. The abuser expects his victim to crumble. So many times, they do.

I don't like the part that came out in this final round. The Girl with the Dragon Tattoo-ish warrior part that will defend mercilessly if needed. I remember thinking to myself: He looks scared. Oh wait, I'm scaring him with what I am saying. He believes me. He knows I am strong enough and that, if pushed hard enough, I will. I'm not afraid of a fight and a rebuild. That's part of the magic, realizing that I had already been through the hard part. And if I can survive that, I can survive anything. I did not end up having to.

He felt that strength and didn't push me further. He knew the antics wouldn't work on me anymore. I was stronger. I couldn't be thrown. I was "momma bear," and those cubs are not going to suffer because of us. No fucking way. We are done. This is done.

On September 23rd, I got the signed divorce papers back from the judge. On September 25th, I moved in. I closed on my new home, the one the boys and I built out together and picked together.

The final moving day came. The day I permanently left the home I had created with love, leaving behind my belongings, my cats, everything except for my clothes, and a few personal effects. It was the only home the boys ever knew, and where I was no longer safe. That same day, I moved into a new home I created for the boys and me in our new chapter, created with love, the Hive's collective effort, and hope for us as a family.

On that day, before doing anything else, I went to the grassy park area where Richard and his dog used to play every day, laughing and enjoying time with their canine and human friends. He loved spending time there so very much. I sat down on the bench where he used to sit, holding an urn of his ashes and the crystals I had been carrying through the whole ordeal, watching the sunrise. "Thank you," I said to him, tears streaming down my face. "Thank you for helping me to get here. I promise you, I promise you, I will never, ever go back."

Now, looking back, I understand why when he said he knew he wouldn't live to 60, he was right. I wish he had been wrong. I wish he was still here. I wish we could talk. But I am grateful. I am grateful to have experienced his support, his love, his wisdom, his weakness, and his vulnerability. His admiration, his defense of me, and his devotion were far greater than I deserved. He dropped a tear of light into a very dark place, and it was enough for me to see my way out.

Years later, he is still with me, looking out for me. I light a white candle, put on some calm music, sit on the patio or the balcony, and we talk. My guardian angel. I can feel hands rubbing my shoulders, comforting me, telling me I will be okay. Reminding me how far I've come, how I can keep going. We laugh and cry together about my woes. He smiles and chuckles at my shenanigans, my work escapades, my hopes, and my dreams. He delights in the advancement of the kids, their joys, and their growth. He gets excited about my crazy ideas, as he always has. I know he still believes in me, which helps me have the courage to continue to believe in myself.

Back to the story. . .

After a few moments of quiet, I take a deep breath, stand up, and walk forward into my new life.

I visit the boys at the house. They have been working with their tutor on a scientific exercise, the metamorphosis of the butterfly. She must know what's been happening. That day, moving day, is the day we are set to release the butterflies in the backyard. As we do, I am reminded of the metamorphosis phase. The step before the butterfly emerges is the step of total liquidation. Safe in the cocoon, she breaks down into her most basic elements before re-emerging as this beautiful creature with wings, who can fly. The symbolism as we are talking about it, watching the butterflies leave the cage and migrate to the flowers in the yard on that sunny day, does not escape me.

Build and Lean on Your Hive

That night and the next day, my nanny, her husband, their kids, and their family members worked all day long unpacking and setting up my new home. A truck delivered all the stuff I bought to furnish and completely restock our lives. Tutti had done an amazing job of coordinating as the operations lead, managing all of this. There's no way I could have pulled this off without her. She managed the whole thing, and I was just a pair of hands (maybe half a pair of hands even). My sister came to town, and there were other helpers, too.

At five o'clock that Saturday, the 26th of September, my kids walked into a receiving line of people clapping and cheering, saying, "Welcome to your new home," and showing them up to their new playroom upstairs with toys and games and familiar objects for them to play with. Like a fairy tale, instead of what could easily have been a nightmare, we started to settle into our new home.

That example was the Hive in action. The Hive that I had built of people that I cared for and supported in the ways that I could. Instead of being ashamed of taking a village approach as an indication of my poor mothering abilities, I felt a tremendous sense of gratitude, relief, and joy. I feel so fortunate for that because this story would have been totally different. Had it not been for the kids, I would have been dead. Had it not been for the Hive, the kids would have been traumatized. And had it not been for the journey, the prophecy would have been fulfilled, another generation on their way.

Through all the stuff, all the steps, all the twists and turns, the Hive was there to support and carry me when I couldn't carry myself, even if it was for just a step. You don't have to do it alone. In fact, doing so leads to worse outcomes. **Build and lean on your hive.**

Phase 3: Reflection and Journaling

Journal Exercise

- Think back to the example of the early cognitive dissonance that starts to occur. In reflection on your own experiences, when can you identify the early signs of toxicity?

  _____

  _____

  _____

  _____

- Reflecting on the HiveStrong tools of recovery, what is an example of a tool you have used in your life? What tools could you benefit from using? (Oxygen Mask on You First, Build & Lean on Your Hive, etc.)

  _____

  _____

  _____

  _____

PHASE 4

SUCCESS-ISH

CHAPTER 12

SPRINT THROUGH THE FINISH

"All we have to do now, is take these lies and
make them true somehow... Freedom"
–George Michael

It took four and a half months to get divorced. And it was a sprint. It was in the middle of Covid; it was insane. When you're running that fast, you don't just stop when the divorce is final; you keep running at full speed, which I did. Right into a cement wall.

*I was energized by my new sense of freedom, the accomplishments, and the support, and excited to see what new possibilities would lead to. **Eighteen again**. On my own. Wounded. Rebuilding. Something to prove, something to hide, something to run from, something to fill the familiar gaping hole that gripped my being. I'm in a full sprint. This time, with the critical responsibility of two kids who deserved better.*

I started conceptualizing a practice, started a major construction project at home, and invested in more real estate. I started to gain more professional industry influence. I got elected to the board of a non-profit. I kept going, and it was still the same. I remember crying the day I won a Woman of the Year award. I was very appreciative and grateful, but also still really sad and lonely.

I was definitely in a state of hyper-vigilance and hyper-arousal, always wondering when and who was going to turn, always expecting it.

The toxicity that has been coursing through your veins doesn't just stop after the break from the latest toxic cycle. It goes places. It affects thinking. You make bad decisions, painfully regrettable decisions, during these periods. People are hurt. I've forgiven myself and view that time with compassion, but oof. Suffice it to say, while the external may have looked one way, how I felt and who I felt I was wasn't what I wanted to be. **Not Me.**

I'm dating on and off. I go through phases of exploring what I want and what I'm interested in unapologetically. There is a freedom when newly single— untethered, open to choose what you choose, not having to answer to someone else. The rush that happens. The craziness of the apps. I have amazing stories, and I have horrible stories. Way too much power in my hands to command that kind of attention with such availability. We'll leave these stories for the comedic bit to come later. Single, headstrong, independent, and very open-minded. I was a force to reckon with.

I'm jittery, and I can't quite get the regulation right. I overreact to things, I underreact to things, and I start to get burned out because of all the stuff. I'm trying to do way too much. Between properties and expanding into new areas professionally, I've overextended in life. Just too much to manage. I underestimate demand and overestimate my capability. Needing to prove something and quiet the voice inside my head telling me that I am a worthless whore, never enough, eternally a fuck-up. I can feel the truth of those words in my bones.

I often play music very loudly and dance.

CHAPTER 13

RUBBER ASS

Eighteen months after my divorce, I have a hysterectomy, thinking it will knock me out for a couple of weeks and force me to slow down. I think because it's partial, it will be simple and a fairly easy recovery. I am wrong.

Surgery is painful. Recovery is painful. I am thrown into immediate, full-blown surgical menopause. My blood pressure is all over the place. My regulation is all over the place. I'm having hot flashes, and night sweats are soaking my sheets. I can't eat. My brain is a disaster. I loathe myself for what I'm experiencing. I feel that I'm an awful human being. I don't realize what is happening medically at this point.

I can tell something isn't right, but I can't control it because I judge and shame myself. It never occurs to me that there may be a medical issue happening. I just internalize it as my own defectiveness, familiar self-defeating cognitions back again. Looking back, it's almost comical how that kind of dramatic hormonal shift manifests. I'm quite fortunate my Hive gives me so much support and grace.

Then, an unexpected major setback. I'm thrown straight into the black hole. It's always interesting to see how people respond in those moments. There are those who are fueled by seeing you get hit and go down, and they seek out attempts to twist the knife further, delighting in your pain. This is a key indicator of someone in the dark triad. There are also those who instinctively want to encourage and lift you up, seek out ways to support and accept you for who you are, including who you are not. The upshot is that I'm faced with unexpected life pivots. I'm faced with situations where I have to decide which tool to pull out: brass knuckles or what I would later dub "rubber ass."

These are the two main options when you get gut-punched; doing nothing isn't one of them. There is an energy and a force you have to contend with. Do I stand up and punch back hard? Or do I go with the force, allow myself to fall, and bounce off of my rubber ass, making that velocity work to my advantage? It's a strategic question, really. What is going to lead to the best outcome the quickest? What is most aligned with my true north? Is the fight and energy worth it? What do I need to radically accept? What really matters here? These are all critical questions that allow me to move through the first key steps of the HiveStrong process quickly.

Setbacks during the recovery process can be re-traumatizing and re-trigger those negative cognitions, which is part of why survivors can often experience them more acutely and struggle with more severity. PTSD can bring a hyper-arousal state that makes the situation or experience even worse. Giving yourself some grace and patience and understanding what is happening, really enables the continued and deeper work that is needed to ultimately heal and thrive. It is also not unusual during this vulnerable time for you to still be gravitating toward and attracting toxic people. You still have toxins raging through your veins, affecting your own decisions and behavior. You have more toxic experiences, which feed the self-defeating and deserving narrative that still exists. There is almost a nostalgia in the familiarity of being in this place, spent and depleted, with parts of you pointing to the most recent evidence of these narratives in your mind.

The good news is that **each trigger is a treasure map:** Each one of those toxic narratives that get sparked up in your mind points the way for your recovery. Each one is a "tell" about a trauma wire that needs to get tagged and eradicated. Identifying them, examining them, and understanding them gives you the intel you need to execute.

CHAPTER 14

REPEATING CYCLES

Do the Work, Then Do It Again (Again)

I keep pushing forward, in search of peace, love and success, but find myself back at square one again. Around, around, and around we go. It's like being on a Ferris wheel, watching the same scenes play over and over again. Moving but not really going anywhere. Same twisted path, same twisted pain, same twisted ending. Round and round we go. And all alone again.

What is the draw? Why repeat the cycle? It's like an internal dance, a sexy bachata dance with a part that wants you to fail, to fall, to self-destruct, and to self-loathe. That part of you takes such great satisfaction in your destruction. She is fueled by it. Energized by it. Like a satiated vampire. It's a familiar seductive pull, longing, belonging. Even a comfort as you know it's true, it's deserved, it's who you really are.

It's so hard not to surrender to that part of yourself. Where does it come from? I'm not sure yet, but I have an idea.

I'm better now at the intervention, the self-compassion that's needed. Better at not making decisions that take the spiral and build a hurricane in my life. I'm keeping my doctor's appointments. Now, if I could just keep getting my labs done on time. 🧛‍♀️ ⚕️

Now, I'm better at pulling back and reminding myself to be kinder. The kinder I am to myself, the kinder I'll be to others, and the more I'll ultimately get done and impact.

I keep reminding myself I'm doing amazing work. I'm making a positive impact on people's lives. I have no idea how the fuck this happened. How I possibly could have accomplished this. I see so much I'm not doing, where I'm falling short, how I suck in so many ways. God damn, I just want to shake this fucking narrative. I clearly have more to do. I'm trying to remind myself I'm a badass and bring forward a gift. I have to remind myself that the boys feel loved and are taken care of. It's not perfect, but that's okay. They are learning resilience and flexibility—all good things for kids to learn to be successful.

One night, as I'm in full-on self-loathing, processing another failing relationship, almost in disbelief at what has transpired, my beautiful friend sends me a text telling me it's getting easier to get up every day. It's such a welcome note, really perfectly timed. I'm so happy she is walking her path, as she deserves to be free. It is a hard journey, for sure. Her courage in walking through and the moment of sending me some inspiration does the trick.

I remind myself that I'm doing the hard, real work, and I'm getting there. It's harder to face and deal with the pain than it is to stuff it into a box. Anyone can pull that move. Anyone can be that tough, grisly exterior. Anyone can spend their life running and hiding from themselves, secretly licking their wounds as they deny them, and then wrap their identity and life patterns around that core avoidance. Anyone can damage relationship after relationship and other human beings with their own unresolved crap. Anyone can pretend. "The hard way's hard, but not nearly as hard as the easy way."

I need to keep doing the real work. I need to acknowledge what is there. Let myself cry, sob, and scream. Question myself, blame myself, hate myself, and be horrified by it all. Angry. Exhausted. Let's pull out the emotions wheel, as there is a lot I can identify here. Purge the toxin.

And then accountability.

I ask myself the hard questions while being compassionate about the answers. Why did I connect with this person? What did I overlook or gloss over? What need was I trying to fill? How did I feed and fuel what happened here?

How could I be okay with someone demanding I call them every night when traveling to ensure I am not cheating? How am I still talking to someone who asks me for money? Why is this person always criticizing me? Disparaging me? Where is that feeling in my stomach coming from? Why is my head spinning, my thoughts racing? How can I be here again?

There is good news. I'm not in the same place. I recognize it earlier. I call it out earlier. I see myself reacting and being all dysregulated. I know where that comes from. I blunt and fight back.

Sometimes in these situations, I use my brass knuckles and punch hard; sometimes, I let myself fall and focus on bouncing back up. It depends on which strategy makes the most sense. But in each instance, I learn, map, attack, and eradicate my own poison, learning how to sustain myself through.

Oxygen Mask on You First

After the ten semi-trucks have run over me and I've cried all the tears—throat raw from screaming, arms tired from punching, hands torn from grabbing—I pick myself up and start to run a bath. A hot bath, dim light, candle-lit, calm music playing, the right salts and scents to soothe my mind. Slipping my tired, worn, hurt body and soul into the water, and soaking. After a while, I start to care for my body and scrub away a layer. It's the last part of pulling out the toxins within and letting them go. After all the right parts are relaxed, soft, and buffed, I rinse off and come out fresh and renewed, ready to face what's next.

During these phases, I encounter situations professionally as well. It's just the reality of life. Companies are full of people. Hurt people hurt people. Shit happens. I start to see how the pattern plays out: regardless of which category of life the toxic relationship happens to fall in, the playbook is the same. My navigation and internal responses improve. I follow the steps I've developed, and it works. It leads to better outcomes and more successes.

No. I'm not in the same place. I'm not the same person. I have walked through total fucking hell. This ain't shit in comparison. I can get through this. I'm not giving xxx that kind of power over me. F#ck that. I'm almost insulted just by the arrogance of that thought. I have to keep the oxygen mask on. Keep taking care of myself. Take my health seriously. Prioritize it, especially in these types of destabilizing moments. Keep the mask on and turn up the air when needed. That is what keeps the boys happy, healthy, and well taken care of by the Hive with two loving parents. And that is really all that matters.

How Do You Turn Triggers Into Treasure? (Triggers Are a Treasure Map of Recovery)

Once you are able to clearly identify your triggers, and your physical response when they are getting activated, you can make your plan of attack to mitigate their detrimental impact while taking the necessary steps for permanent removal, just as you would with any other medical, progressive condition.

That increased physiological self-awareness can become a significant strategic advantage while treating and working through recovery. Living life, having a career, having children, interacting with human beings and the world means running into potentially damaging experiences everywhere. No human being is immune. A radical acceptance of that reality is required. Successful outcomes do not come from becoming stuck on that truth and being destabilized each time. They come from moving into a Bobby Fischer mindset and taking smart actions that proactively deliver the best possible outcome, accounting for the realities.

Recognizing your body when you first start to become activated makes it possible to maintain a higher level of executive function, as you are not in full-on lizard brain yet. That is where I learned to blunt the impact and where you can too. When I waited too long and ignored what was happening, the severity and negativity of the outcome increased. But I could prevent that from happening through increased self-awareness and smart, mitigating actions.

Learning this trick made a huge difference during this stage of recovery. To fully eradicate things, I would need to pull out a bigger gun for that work, like EMDR or another tool in the toolkit. And I do. The parallel path of managing and combatting the PTSD response was the winning combination. When I was triggered, thinking that someone was doing me dirty—**you are a worthless whore to be used, exploited, and discarded**—it helped me to pause and ask the right questions. What evidence do I see of what is happening? What is my body telling me? Who are my thought partners who can give me perspective? What outcome do I most want here? What is the best response?

Do the Work, Then Do It Again

The process is not linear. It takes work and practice to really love and accept who you are, including who you are not. This is a crucial part of this journey, inward work that continues today.

I remember talking in great depth about addiction and recovery with Richard and later, another recovering addict that I would have a serious relationship with. Both of them were active in AA/NA, respectively. There was probably a reason I gravitated to them both and sought to learn from their recovery journey.

One thing I admired about both recovery programs was how they allowed for the complex reality of life as an addict. The crazy shit that happens. The highs and lows. The fucked-up thinking. Recovery from addiction requires admitting and accepting powerlessness over the addiction while taking full accountability for the recovery. That duality, understanding and appreciating that, and walking those steps is what makes a survivor rather than someone who is still in a victim state.

The reason I often say, "It's a journey inward first" in this phase is that triumph comes through that self-healing, and it's not a linear process. Our external state manifests from our internal state. We must go inward and heal the foundation. It is the only path. There are relapses that will occur. There are successful moments. They are all okay. After all, it is the human experience.

Phase 4: Success-ish Reader Reflection

Journal Exercise

- What were the important HiveStrong tools used in this section?

  _____

  _____

  _____

  _____

- What tools have you used, and which ones do you think you should incorporate?

  _____

  _____

  _____

  _____

PHASE 5

PURPOSE

CHAPTER 15

YOU GOT TO GIVE IT TO KEEP IT

Richard was eight years sober. I remember watching him get that eight-year coin with so much pride. I remember seeing the community within AA and how people supported each other. He taught me a lot through sharing his own recovery journey and learning what those steps looked like for him, what they meant to him, and his recovery. The falls that inevitably happen along the way. He sponsored people and became very active in AA.

When I asked, "Why are you so active and involved in AA? What do you get out of dedicating so much of your time, energy, and life to it?" He smiled and said, "You gotta give it to keep it." He meant that helping others with their journey reinforced and strengthened his own, and it gave him purpose.

When I put my professional lens on this, I see the scientific brilliance in this approach as well. The best way to learn a concept and build a skill is to teach it to someone else. So much so that I've used it as part of corporate training processes for onboarding and upskilling both technical and leadership skills across numerous populations, called a "teach-back." I think this plays out spiritually and karmically as well. What you receive back through giving is on a very high multiple. Talking to people in philanthropic work, I often found that they will quickly agree.

The situations reminded me of my personal experience during the pandemic. How I was leading the human side of the crisis in business, juxtaposed to what was happening in my personal life. How I became acutely aware of my privilege and advantage on so many levels, so many fronts. I have civil litigation experience in my professional life. I had a career, so I knew I had my own source of income to stand up on, even if I lost everything. I had people in my orbit who were very supportive. I had intel or things that were really impactful and led to a quick and successful divorce. I had a team around me to carry some of the weight of the orchestration of it all. I had buffers in place that gave some protection. I knew, from those early days in my adulthood, what it was like when you don't have those things. And I had an acute, daily reminder of what that was like as we progressed through the months of the pandemic and the complete upheaval and trauma that caused our employees. I knew that I had the boys wrapped in a bubble, very unlike what most people experience in life. What I didn't know at the time was **why.**

As I moved through recovery and started sharing excerpts of the journey, when appropriate, I found that it was empowering for others to hear. By openly sharing my journey so boldly and honestly, it gave courage to others to continue or start their own. My story was intel, just like my friends' story had been. My open acknowledgment of my own fallibility and humanity, balanced with accountability, fueled my soul.

A year after the divorce was final, a very close friend of mine who had given me critical intel at the beginning, before I even knew I was in an abusive cycle, contacted me. She was still deeply in the throes of her multi-year devastating divorce, on the brink of bankruptcy. The kids were a mess. Everything was a mess. She was currently $20,000 into the attorneys. The judge was telling them they needed to get this deal done, or they were going to trial. The attorneys were saying, "Pay up before we do anything further." He had a horrible proposal on the table, engineered to minimize support, not in the best interests of the *children. She was completely beside herself and considering accepting his terms with no other plausible choice. She asked me for a loan.*

This was the first situation where I realized: Wait a minute, I can really, really make an impact here. I can give back to somebody who gave so much to me and doesn't even realize what she's done. I had a final bit of unallocated cash from my settlement. I said to her, "Okay, are you ready? Are you really ready to fight? When I punch, I wear brass fucking knuckles. One and done, motherfucker. Are you ready to fucking fight for you and these kids?? If we do this, you cannot wilt halfway through because he is going to fight back. This is your life, and you call the shots. I am loaning you cash, but it does not mean I will make any decisions here. I just want to make sure I am making a winning investment. I am very happy to do so, and I find it very fitting to use the final unallocated cash from the divorce for this exact purpose. You have no idea how much insight and intel I got from you sharing your story back in Fort Lauderdale. The way it enabled critical decisions I made. You gotta remember, I'm not in this position because I am better than you in some way. I'm in this position because I have advantages and privileges, many of which other people do not have. I want to use the power for good. Fuck these motherfuckers. Are you ready to fight?"

"Yes," she said.

"Ok then, I'll get with my attorney, we will draw up a contract, and it's "go" time. We can have this done very quickly."

In our first business transaction, I loaned her the money and empowered her in a couple of key moments. This precipitated a shift of power in the case. It went from her being on her knees about to acquiesce to standing up and saying, "No, I am not going to accept these terms. Not only are these not in the best interests of our children, but more so, they would be damaging to them. I am prepared to go to trial."

Discovery begins.

He goes to his toolkit and pulls it out. "I am going to mess with her head, knife her right in the gut, make her crack, make her drink, make her act out in some unhealthy way that I can then use to exploit and control." That's the move. They all use it. Every time.

He shows up unexpectedly at a kids' event. His presence rattles her. She calls me in a panic, shaking, ready to make a bad, trauma-wiring kind of decision. She is beside herself.

Somewhere in the conversation, I remember asking her, "Can you see him right now? Do you see him across the way over there?"

"Yes, he is over there."

"What's he doing? Does he have that smirk, that little baby face and blue eyes, and 'good guy' look? Smug and wooing the crowd?"

"Yes, he is. That fucker! He is."

"Those are all your friends he is yucking it up with, right? To fuck with you? Knowing it's fucking with you?"

"Yeah. That's exactly what he is doing."

"Okay. Alright. That's okay. I'm glad that motherfucker is here. Now I want you to look at him and just keep your eyes on him, watching while I talk for a minute. Can you do that?"

"Yes, I can do that."

"Ok, great. Watch that smile on his face—good guy laugh. All full of himself right now because he knows you are in a panic right now. Smiling and laughing, wooing your friends to question why you would ever want to leave such a sweet and amazing guy. I can see him in my mind right now. Are you watching him? Are you seeing that?"

"Yes, I see it. I'm watching him. That motherfucker. What an asshole for showing up here tonight."

"Yes, he really is. But you know what? I'm so glad he did. He is clearly rattled by your strength, so he is doing the one thing, the only thing his pathetic ass can do. He has no real leverage, no real justifiable position behind his proposal, and he has been unable to break you to accept it. So what is that motherfucker doing? He is showing up here to fuck with your mind. The only power he actually has is to destabilize you and get you to do something to self-

destruct that he can exploit and use as leverage. That is his only fucking power because he is a weak, pathetic piece of shit motherfucker. Are you looking at him? Do you see this?"

"Oh my God, Rachael, oh my God."

"Mmmhmmm, now you see. Now you see how pathetic and weak he is underneath that bullshit facade. We know what's up. Now, I want you to imagine him in front of us on his knees while hearing my voice telling him exactly what he is. Can you see that?"

"Yes, ha! I can see that."

"Good. Now, I want you to imagine we are peering deep into his eyes. He knows we know his truth; we are telling him. He is begging for mercy, begging for forgiveness. Begging for us to be kind."

"Oh my God."

"And you know what we are going to do? We can do anything we want to him. He is weak, on his knees. He deserves the wrath and degradation that could be hurled his way. We are going to look him dead in the eyes and won't even say the words, 'Not worth it.' Our eyes will send the message with our recognition of the truth before them. Then, we are going to turn around, and walk away, and go have some fun. Are you ready to do that with me?"

"Yes, I am."

"Ok, let's do it."

And with that exercise, we had a very good laugh and adult woman-like giggle.

"I want you to fucking suck it up, take a deep breath, and I want you to walk your ass over and have fun with your friends. And if it starts to shake you up a little bit again, just go back to that visualization."

With that, we end the conversation. She stands up, walks back over, and starts laughing, having fun with her friends. She is strong, her head is held high, and she is calm and in control. This freaks him out, and guess what? He acts a fool and starts acting out. So much so that it is noticeable to others, which creates a ripple, and all of a sudden, the power dynamic has shifted.

Time for deposition. She's scared. Who wouldn't be? There's plenty riding on depositions. And when you aren't used to being in legal processes, the formality and language can be very intimidating. We prepare. We talk about all the dark things she is afraid of. I reassure her that the lawyers, the judge, the court reporter—they are all probably closet freaks. No one cares about that. They don't care about the kids, the sex, the emotions. They care about dividing the assets and their own sense of importance in the process. We work through some grounding processes to use in preparation and during. It's still Covid, so the proceedings are on Zoom. You can hold something in your hands to help you smile and stay calm that no one can see. Box breathing. Taking sips of water to pause and breathe. Buffering the meetings with self-care. There is a whole toolkit to pull from to customize.

She nails the deposition. He flounders his. Game fucking over. Checkmate. Within a month, a much more fair, balanced parenting agreement, more in line with the best interests of the children, was agreed upon, assets divided, and a decree signed by a judge. No trial ever became necessary. Only the strength and will to do what was necessary for the kids.

There's more to this story. But through that experience of supporting someone and the ways that I could support her—after she had supported me in the ways that she could—that's where HiveStrong was born. I realized the power of sharing those experiences, of the encouragement, of the coaching, of the right resources, and of pulling other people in at times to wrap around that person. I realized how we each bring something to the hive, and we each take something as well. It is reciprocal. It is a collective community dedicated to empowering and lifting each other.

The more I listened to the universe, built my skills, educated and certified myself, the more I stayed on track with my own self, my own journey, and the things that brought me through. It gave use and purpose to the investments, to the privilege, and to the platform. It's where pain becomes purpose.

I start to hone the steps, working with more people "on the side of the desk": here and there, when possible, as this is not a source of income, and I have a career. This is about inspiration, healing, and purpose, giving me time and space to develop the right model, balanced with the other important priorities in my life.

Time and time again, no matter where I am (plane, beach, spa, date), I continue to run into survivors on their own path. I continue to have survivors who want to introduce me to other people on their journey who haven't quite hit the survivor stage to help them get out of their current abusive situations. I am starting to listen as the universe speaks.

Now I'm coaching, and the hive is in action. We are assisting people with the right referrals and resources to help them navigate out. And many of them do. We are helping people who are already out but aren't in recovery—they are coping. There are many reasons why it takes a woman, on average, seven attempts to leave her abuser. Those are real factors, not about strength of will, that have to be dealt with in order to break free. My background in operations and HR in restaurants brings a certain set of skills that helps people through transitions to land on their feet. I always root for the underdog: resilient and with something to prove. I feel more and more like: Okay, this is absolutely my purpose.

I had discovered my superpower: creating safe spaces and communities with reciprocating value, especially because I talk about the things people are afraid to talk about. For sex abuse survivors, in particular, this is an incredibly powerful and healing moment to experience. I also learned, in the backyard, through these deeply connecting experiences together, with the candles lit, fireplace on, waterfall flowing, and food and drink, how empowering it was for others to listen, demonstrate openness and acceptance, and create psychological safety by strategically sharing parts of my story: the failures, darkness, and insecurities, just as much as the successes and how they happened. I saw people transform. I saw how it helped them in their journey of awakening and purpose. I saw how I was giving them the same gift my hive had given me: Purpose.

CHAPTER 16

GOODBYE - - - -!

Get Rid of the Monster in Your Belly

A close friend of mine comes to spend some time at the hive refuge. I'm spending as much time there as I can, doing my job, building toward the future, working through the cycles, getting better, relapsing less, and persevering.

We are sitting on the balcony one morning, drinking coffee, listening to the waves, reflecting on her most recent battle. She, too, knows what it's like when the scars go as deep as the beginning, and the wound has been numbed in oh so many different ways. I'm in a certain mood—call it "defiant reverence." I'm thinking about my momma bear instinct as we are talking. It is another stark example of the trauma caused by an unavailable and unwell mother and how that leads to repeated cycles of trauma through life experiences, ultimately manifesting in self-harm along the way.

I'm trying to explain to her how utterly unacceptable her experience is. How the treatment she received was so far from what a loving, healthy mother does for her child. How incomprehensible it is to me that someone could ever allow those things to happen to their child, much less foster the situation and continue the damage.

In my typical shock jock fashion, I say to her, "Look, let me explain it this way. If I ever found out that someone had done to my child what had been done to you, my visceral impulse would be to rip off their head and _____, _____, and _____." I have a unique and creative thinking ability in this area. She looks at me with shock that I even put that together. It's my own special version of Cards Against Humanity.

I laugh and tell her, of course, I wouldn't do anything violent. I'm just putting words to the natural, human, motherly instinct and how strong, barbaric, and protective that instinct is. I want you to remember that the next time you try to rationalize or justify your mother's actions. There is a huge difference between understanding why someone is the way they are and being at peace with that truth without holding onto anger. You don't have to gaslight yourself as to its nature to be able to accept it.

Then we decide, fuck it, we are at the ocean. Let's apply that ridiculous thinking to some visualization and maybe rid ourselves of the hold that this person has over her. I have my own things that hold on me too. Certain people, certain situations, and certain narratives that circle around like a loop.

So, we decide to visualize her mother. How does she see her? Where in her body does she feel activated?

"She's a woodpecker," she says. "On my shoulder. Trying to peck into my brain." Ohh, I like that image. I ask her, "Okay, do you want to break her neck or drown her in the ocean?"

She laughs and says, "Drown her in the ocean."

"Let's do it," I say.

So we get ourselves ready and head down to the beach. It's a beautiful afternoon. Light breeze, sun shining, not too hot. The reflection of the sun looks like diamonds sparkling on the ocean. There are a few other sunbathers hanging out.

We set up our chairs, get settled in for a minute, relax, and take in the scene. After a few minutes relaxing to the sounds of the waves, I ask her if she's ready to do it. She says yes.

We make our way out into the waves. We go out probably 50ish feet from shore. My neighbors can see us, but they can't hear us. It's not too deep. We can *catch some of the waves. We start laughing and talking about the ridiculousness of what we are doing, but we're going to do it anyway. She's been self-destructing and having a really hard time with this current round of traumatizing interactions. She's been attacking it with all sorts of interventions and care. What is the worst thing that could happen? We collapse in giggles like little girls playing.*

So we are out, bouncing in the waves, enjoying the scenery, laughing, and we decide it's time. I get serious for a moment. "Okay, let's take a look at your mother. Do you see her there?" I ask.

"Yes, she's here."

"What does she look like?"

"She's a woodpecker."

"What is she doing?"

"She's trying to peck into my brain. She won't stop."

"Okay. Are you ready? Time to drown that bitch in some waves. We are going to jump under the wave when the right one comes, swim through it, and come up on the other side. And when we do, we are going to throw our hands in the air and scream, 'Goodbye c*$+ mother!' Do you understand?" I take a moment and demonstrate, reiterating my instructions.

She says, "Yes."

So we do it. We find the right-size wave that will crest at the right time in front of us, and we jump through it, swimming hard, feeling the pull of the wave in the other direction, powering through. We come up the other side, jump out of the ocean like mermaids, and yell through our giggles, "GOODBYE MOTHERF&*KER." We collapse in laughter, letting ourselves bobble in the now-calm water.

After recovering, I ask her if she wants to do it again. She says, "YEAH!" So we do it again, and then again, and again. After a while, we are spent and just continue to float, feeling lighter, released, safe, almost overcome by the beauty of the ocean and sun before us. We are grateful.

We jokingly dub this the "Goodbye $%^+! HiveStrong Ritual," and I start to dissect its potential value as part of the process. She is visiting another friend in a moment of key transition from a vicious abuser or negative cognition that has hijacked her brain. They don't have the ocean, but they have food, pictures, and a fire. They use their tools and burn some things in effigy and burn the pictures. Purge the toxin. Watch it incinerate into ash. Breathe.

They do the ritual the night before she moves out for good. It's cathartic. It's sad. It's funny. It's ridiculous. It's crude. It is all those things. So are the things that have happened to you. Letting go of that dream that you hang onto for dear life is not at all easy.

Since then, a few different iterations of this ritual have been done. It's not the be-all and end-all, but it is definitely worth including. It is one of many tools in the toolbox that, along the journey, are so helpful to take the next step. That's part of the key to success: going one step at a time. Sometimes it's a small one, sometimes it's a big one. Sometimes, it's best to keep your head down and just focus on making each one. Sometimes, you have to lift your head up and make sure you are still going in the right direction.

But all along the way, it is important to let go of that pain and burden you are carrying. It's only weight that slows you down. And the only way to do it is to face each one head-on and eradicate it using whatever tools you need. I'm okay that my neighbors were looking at us slightly puzzled. It's not for everyone.

CHAPTER 17

SURRENDER TO THE UNIVERSE

When the Universe Speaks, Listen

I'm learning to listen, really listen… and trust. A lifelong faithful atheist who finds herself cracking a smile while saying, "Just go with God." What do I know? I'm always waiting for the curtain to pull back on life, reality to walk on stage to say, "Just kidding," while sucker-punching the breath out of me. It's a play I've been in a few times.

When Opportunities to Stretch and Grow Present Themselves, Step into Them

Even when—scratch that—*especially* when there are big stretches with big growing pains, that's the moment before the breakthrough that never would have happened otherwise. Sure, you can stay where you are, thinking that staying "there" somehow brings safety and security. I just haven't ever found real safety or security in that place. In fact, it's where I've found the exact opposite of security and where the frantic attempt to hold onto something that was never there to begin with ensues. Evolution and strength happen when we adapt, not when we stand still.

Recently, I've come to realize the superpower that exists within survivors. We become strong warriors of a sort. There is magic, a truth, a strength, and a resiliency that only comes from walking that path. From experiencing life and everything in it shattering like a mirror that explodes into a thousand sharp pieces in your face, cutting you to a place of unrecognizability, not once, but over and over again, maybe every time you look. Finally, the makeup, mascara, and bravado don't cover it up anymore, and you fall to your knees. You bleed. You cry. You fuck shit up. You cut yourself worse. You scar. And then, slowly, you take a deep breath and stand back up. You tenderly put bandages on the wounds. You fight for yourself. And you build the next chapter in your life.

Why don't you stay down and wallow, cry, bleed? Why don't you let everyone else attend to your wounds, act on your behalf, or make your decisions? Why don't you do that? It would be so much easier. Why? Because you've got shit to do, and those babies of yours matter more than anything, anyone, or any situation, including yours. And they deserve the life you didn't. They deserve happiness, joy, love, and to be safe. They matter more.

Once you've gone through that journey, lived that pain, walked that path, and have come through to the other side, there is truly nothing that you can't come through again. That confidence in the strength of self, grounding in personal truth, that you can always step in, step forward, step through, no matter what, while knowing what truly matters in this existence, vibrates through every cell of your being. With that knowledge and confidence, the decision to step at all, to jump, to risk, to believe in the possibility of yourself and life shifts *dramatically*. And your lens of the universe becomes wider and deeper.

I light a white candle and talk to Richard all the time. I take these big, risky life steps, not really knowing what the next one's going to be, but just having some kind of faith in myself, if only with a dogged determination not to break now. I visualize the life I want to lead. I test and refine the model.

I reframe the hits that happen inevitably in all facets of life—kids, professional, relationships—as moments of learning, messages to hear, things to notice and be present for, things to learn and change, reminding myself of my true north.

This is when the non-profit takes shape. I want to help survivors, not get my income from them. This is the right model. I know this can have a real impact on other people, and that is meaningful. A purpose for my pain and fortune.

In relationships, I tolerate less and less of what I shouldn't. The trauma voice and my inner voice are in a battle to the death with each other.

On one trip, I'm in LA after spending the last couple of days with the boys at Disney and Universal (the first time for both). I've been going back and forth with someone for several months. Not good. I remember saying to him, "Hey, look, you know what? Forget it. I am done with this. I am not perfect, but I'm going to go find the one who is perfect for me. This is not working for me. I really do wish you the best."

It was hard to do, but I was proud of myself for doing it. Breaking the pattern earlier on. Stopping the cycle. Paying attention to the signs in my body before my head was fully ready to acknowledge what my body already knew. The mechanisms, tools, and strengths were working. I could see more clinically the wiring that had been tapped into, the cognitions that had been activated, the toxic playbook in action, and the way it impacted my thinking. I still saw and experienced that thinking, but I was getting stronger and more powerful in fighting it back, and I was seeing the progress.

I took a deep breath, looked up to the stars, and dreamed.

CHAPTER 18

PAIN TO PURPOSE

As the months pass, other challenges happen, other ups and downs. But what also becomes clear is the reasoning and channel for it all. The incredibly rewarding HiveStrong work. The continued messages the universe keeps sending my way. The journey with the boys, our hive, their neurodivergent diagnosis, how we all work together to learn and navigate how best to help them, while managing through our own.

Their hive works together; we watch them grow, evolve, excel, achieve, and break through. Their individuality starts to emerge. The clichés about parenting and your kids growing up fast are all true. Each step and phase is amazing and challenging in its own right. I am grateful for it all.

I see how HiveStrong helps people in a very real, tangible, and meaningful way. We continue to focus on how to excel in life while paying it forward simultaneously. It's not always easy or perfect, but we learn a ton.

The message from the universe is clear about where to focus energy, what the priorities are, and what the "stuff" and achievements can be used for. I had to be careful because, at times, I didn't take care of my foundation, and it erodes if you don't. I burn out, recover, and discover where my gifts belong. I pay attention to what my body and mind are telling me, the messages I hear, and the signals I see from the universe. The unexpected direction that particular *path takes is petrifying while unabashedly authentic, acknowledging my own truth, maybe for the first time.*

Taking big steps, sometimes getting pushed, towards making the dream a reality. I work on the nuts and bolts, the fundamentals. Getting the back end and front end of an organization done is no easy feat. Maybe it's always going to be a project. Maybe it will take off. Either is okay. I won't know unless I go for it. Regardless, there will be good outcomes, no matter what.

The HiveStrong Model

The model that is developed is based on my own experience, research, collaboration, trial, and refinement. It's based on my professional training and experiences. Empowerment is at the center. There is a toolkit to pull from, a roadmap from awakening to purpose, and a network of support across a variety of needs. The point is empowerment, and what emerges is a collaborative approach that ensures that the survivor makes the decisions on how they want to navigate through. We walk alongside, help to construct pathways, and provide support along the way. But the survivor is the one who has to take the steps.

It works; there are successes to celebrate and realities to face. It's not going to be an easy path. At times, self-doubt can be cruel and crushing, and I invite future proof points to reinforce that voice. The battle rages on, but the scales are tipped in our favor, and the momentum and purpose pulse through my veins.

One by one, the pieces come together, and the full model starts to make sense. Keep walking step by step, keeping the oxygen on high and higher when needed to stay on track.

♪♫ 25

Another unexpected pivot, this time a different type of health scare. It's real, it's preventable, and eerily familiar. Except I'm in a different role, consumed by pain in my abdomen, guided by stubborn independence, and annoyed that plans are disrupted. The boys and I were going to be starting our first road trip on Monday, after all.

Now I'm bent over in pain. People encourage me to go to the hospital, but no one is stronger than my own stubborn voice. Thirty hours in, I hear Richard's voice saying, "Rachael, don't wait, go in now. Don't you remember? Don't forget. Don't be foolish and stubborn; take yourself into the hospital tonight." But Tutti's on vacation, and she always steps up when asked. I don't want to do that to her. She deserves her time off uninterrupted. I'm resolute on that fact. I hear him repeat himself in my mind again.

I think back to 2020 and reminisce about our last conversation the night before he died. I said, "I'm so glad it's not Covid! But it's something. Maybe you should go see a doctor?" He said, "Yes, I'll rest this weekend and go Monday if I'm not feeling better by then. Don't you worry about me, Rachael. Go have fun with your friends and enjoy yourself for a while. I'll rest here with Gavin." I was so caught up in my own turmoil that I accepted that plan almost thoughtlessly. A catastrophic decision made in an instant.

We texted after that a couple of times in the morning. I wish I had come out of my own head more and pushed him to go in right then. I underestimated the significance of the symptoms, and as a healthy man often does, he underestimated them, too. It was 100% preventable if caught in time—lethal if not. The symptoms can be nothing, or they can take your life. I remember my grief and regret that I hadn't pushed. It took me so long to let that go.

I don't want the person in my life to look back and think the same thing. I don't want the boys to grow up early, having to handle on their own a mother who is incapacitated or worse. It would be stupid and selfish to subject them to that.

"Go in now, Rachael! Don't wait!" he says, slightly exasperated. I can hear Richard so clearly as I am bent over in pain. I can see that annoyed look on his face, arms gesturing as he talks. He repeats himself again. "Okay! Okay!" I reply.

With that decision, I text my neighborhood teenage babysitter, "Can you come? I think I need to go to the ER." She replies, "On my way." She's been with me since I moved here. A survivor too. We understand each other. She knows that when a cat shows her pain, it's very real.

I drive myself to the hospital where I've had both my babies and then had baby-making removed over these past 14 years. I've got a playlist going, the subwoofer on, helping me make the 20-minute drive down. In retrospect, it was also foolish. I should have had someone else drive, but I was again stubbornly hanging onto independence for all of dear life.

I get to the hospital in one piece, share the news with the people who need to know it, and prepare for what is next. Surgery, recovery, and a slowdown— dear lord, is this real?

The next 36 hours are a haze of anesthesia, painkillers, and managing the systems during the immediate aftermath of the internal cleanup in the hospital. The boys come to visit, adjustments to plans kick into gear, and the unplanned recovery journey begins.

Three weeks earlier, I had been through an EMDR intensive, maybe the most intensive of them all. We got to Pigtails' pain and her trauma, starting to create her safe space. We released some important toxins, but some are still lingering in there.

The combination of the two, while in mid-spin on professional projects, creates yet another clarifying moment of the journey and an example of the HiveStrong process and tools at play.

Tutti has her vacation, as she needs and deserves. She works hard, is dedicated, puts in so much more, and has played such a role in the boys' lives. There are others in the hive who can step up and provide support, too. Not only are they there, but it also helps them in meaningful ways. The relationship needs to be balanced, reciprocal, reliable, and safe.

I reach out to the community and get more childcare help in Texas so I can still spend time with the boys. We get them into camp and make all the arrangements around it. We still get to Florida with the team activating on both sides and on the way, too. The pieces amazingly fall into place while Momma heals. The boys are happy, creating amazing memories, building connection and resilience as we do. I'm putting the oxygen mask on first, leaning on the hive and its reciprocal nature. We continue to support each other, encourage, walk alongside, and show up. The darkness still comes, but this time, I'm able to blunt it and reverse course. I see it and don't avoid it; I just don't let it take over and win.

Amanda comes down, as she often does, to take care of me and keep me company while I recover and write. Now, out of the darkness of the first week, the change in scenery has taken effect. We spend our time resting and chilling, enjoying the authenticity of our friendship, and reflecting a lot. We talk about the "goodbye ritual" with a good laugh and debrief on its effect. Maybe it's time for another; we shall see about that.

The process and the tools are alive in action. I remind myself why they exist, push myself to use them, listen to the hive when they lean in, and take my own medicine. It works. I navigate through.

Because I take that medicine, I am able to navigate through, and to better outcomes. It's a new threshold, a new space, a new beginning, and a new vulnerability that comes with this level of openness. "Opening up the kimono," one of my bosses used to say. Surrendering to the universe, indeed.

CHAPTER 19

THE TRUE TRIUMPH

Sitting on the balcony at the Hive Refuge, we listen to the ocean waves, with soft music playing and the stars and moon providing the light. We talk about the boys—how unique and special they are. How "M" is showing leadership, resilience, and fortitude despite his challenges. How brilliant "A" is, and how he will likely be a scientist. We discuss the people we know who are locked in toxic struggles, and I share what I am working on with my current projects to help other survivors. We ponder what is to come.

I can tell he is reminiscing about our shared love of the ocean, the connection we feel to the somatic sound of the waves, and the desire to retire on the beach (or at least semi-retire). I've done it without him.

I feel bad because he doesn't fully understand what I am saying. He doesn't understand how it applies or maybe doesn't want to. He thinks it is all about the early years. In some ways, that's true. It's where the foundation was laid, but it's not the only part. He is not all to blame. He is not all monster. He is a good dad and cares. I am not an innocent victim with no accountability. That's part of the journey: relearning your voice, acknowledging your truth, and taking accountability for your own actions and recovery. No one is all bad or all good. Anyone can bring out the barbarian when faced with the right set of circumstances. That's part of why it's so hard. We are complex creatures as human beings.

Somehow, he knows that he is safe. That it is not my intention to harm. That I don't want to blow up the life and experience for the boys that we have collectively, successfully created through it all. That I don't hold onto hate and pain. And there is the effect of the refuge itself: the safety, the warmth, the healing environment. The somatic nature of it all has an impact here too.

It's been a few months of pivots and turns, messages and continued learning, that I have navigated while I work on this book. I think about the title that I've had for a long time, struggling with one of the words. What is triumph? I know what it's not, that's for sure. In so many ways, I don't feel like I have triumphed. And I know it's not what I thought it would be. What is *true* triumph?

Back to the story…

I can't ignore what is still there. I need to do the work again. I still doubt my own mind on some things. I still have that wire that runs deep, and I can feel it activating. She's deep in there, critically reminding me of my fuck ups, telling me I am a worthless whore fuck-up loser, disappointment, a failure. She's there with this smirk on her face, just reminding me without even having to say it. When I fall, when I stand up, when I step forward, when I sleep, she is there. I've tried hard to drown her out, to tell her she's wrong, prove to her she's wrong, pretend she doesn't exist, pretend I don't believe her. I find ways to numb the pain that she taps into. The pain of how I know her words are true. She is always there. She is part of me.

I can point to the kids and how amazing they are and how the hive has just succeeded so brilliantly in giving these guys such a solid foundation, happiness and joy. I can point to the things or the people and what's been impacted by some of my work. The unique and fortunate path my career has taken and the privilege it gives me. Acknowledge that there are tangible things I can feel proud of. But none of that feels like a real triumph, especially not in the context of this title.

I start to think about that part of me, the one that snickers and sneers. I think she's not entirely wrong. In fact, maybe she's right. Maybe I need to stop ignoring her and telling her that she's bad and wrong and stupid. Maybe I need to wrap my arms around her to validate why she feels that way, what makes her think that she's so full of anger and contempt. Maybe she needs a safe space to process that stuff, too, because she doesn't understand why it all happened, either. She's too young to understand. She doesn't have the tools, and she needs a safe space too.

Her voice is strong and has a hold. Sometimes, in the middle of the night, she will wake me up, talking so loudly. Thank God I still have my therapist helping me along this journey.

I finally decide to stop ignoring her. Stop telling her she is wrong. Stop telling her to fuck off. Stop showing her anger and rejection. Instead, this time, I turn towards her and say, "I'm here to listen. Tell me what you want to say. I want to know. It's okay to tell me." I can almost sense a relief in her as she processes my words. This isn't a wicked sneer but a slight glimpse of what feels like an exhale and a sense of incoming relief. Maybe she was stuck in a loop because, instead of processing what was going on, she was shamed for it. Let's see what comes out.

I pull out a chair at the figurative table as an invitation for her to sit. I sit down in my chair. She is now moving with me. She quickly starts to sneer and spew out her poisonous words. "You are a whore. You deserve to be used, exploited, and discarded for the trash that you are. You are stupid. You are ugly. You are a fuck-up. You are a cum dumpster. You are fat. You suck at everything. You are disgusting. You are pathetic." She goes on and on until she's gotten out every last possible insult she can think of. Now that she's spewed her venomous energy, she is spent and visibly tired. She slumps down into her chair. She looks up at me.

I say, "Thank you for getting it all out. I know that wasn't easy. It's okay." She looks at me, slightly confused. She is not her usual combative self. "It really is okay. I have those thoughts about myself sometimes. You are probably right about some of it." Puzzled, she continues to gaze at me in that curious way. She had been ready for a fight. "I know why I think some of those things about myself sometimes. I'm really curious, and I'd like to know if you are willing to share openly: Why do you think those things about me?"

She looks at me, starts to say something, and quickly stops. She takes a deep breath and exhales. Then she says, softly but clearly, momentarily vulnerable, "I don't know." She is genuinely unsure.

Later, we go deeper to find the one in pigtails who is having the nightmares. I hold her hand and comfort her when it's time. Help her work through the root cause of her panic and pain. Let her cry, tremble, and shake in fear while my momma part rocks and comforts her. It's really hard to do this work. But we do it together. And I have the right help.

Maybe the triumph isn't in any of the external accomplishments, and that's why it never feels right to use them as examples, nor are they very satisfying for long. Maybe the triumph is in conquering what's inside: accepting and learning to love all the parts and pieces and starting to glue them back together, healing that core pain in the process. Maybe that becomes the best armor for facing future potential threats to my sanity and ensuring the best possible outcome for those I am responsible for, those who need me to make it happen, for so many reasons. Maybe the real triumph is in shining a bright light on it all, cleaning it out, finally achieving personal peace, and channeling the pain into meaningful purpose. Maybe the appendix bursting and spewing toxins through my abdomen was the universe telling me to pause, do the cleanup, finish the job, and heal. You'll die if you ignore it. Acknowledge and face the pain, and you'll be just fine. The poetry of it is not lost on me. Maybe the triumph is in accepting that you aren't alone, don't have to do it alone, and knowing, in your bones, that you are indeed enough.

Funny how the universe guides some things full circle.

I'm back at the refuge with the boys, watching them giggle in delight. Watching them take an excursion with their dad for adventures, watching another rocketship launch, bonding, and the love that is fostered by shared experiences. It's the thing that really matters.

I realize that none of this would be possible if I hadn't put the oxygen mask on first, done the work repeatedly, and continued to focus on purpose. I know what happens to kids when their parents can't. They deserve better. It's my job to give it to them. I have to keep stepping forward for them, for those who've taken steps with me, who need me to take steps with them, and for those to come.

The true triumph for me is in gluing the pieces back together again and being at peace with what I see in the mirror. Being present and at peace internally allows me to be present and at peace with the boys. Dreaming with them about life in the stars. Knowing and laughing at our inside jokes. Creating those special, core memories of happiness and love. Ensuring that they see how relationships have boundaries, evolve, change, and grow, even when they are deeply toxic at certain points. Ensuring that they see how important it is to protect and care for oneself.

Elevate that to experiencing more joy from helping to ensure they have those same moments with their dad as he seeks to find ways to do the same. Funny, how it really, really works: radical acceptance, focusing on the true north, building and leaning on my hive, doing the work, and surrendering to the universe. How possible it is to be in a state of life transition, yet at peace and contentment.

One of my favorite moments this past year was overhearing "M" talking to one of his male caregivers on FaceTime. Neither of them knew I was right around the corner, putting away laundry. I wasn't trying to eavesdrop, but I quickly paused my work and started to listen. "M" is probably 6 years old at the time, on the spectrum, with a communication/speech disability at the time. Because of my own experience, I've always been very cognizant of teaching them about touch, boundaries, and what to do if someone touches them or wants to touch them inappropriately. It is also not lost on me that special needs kids are especially targeted by predators because of how those disabilities can be exploited to mask the abuse. It's always been a high priority and a source of anxiety. So I'm frozen in place, listening almost in shock to this call. The conversation goes something like this:

M: Hey, I want to talk to you about the other day.
Caregiver: What's up, buddy?
M: You pinched me when I was crying, and it really hurt.
Caregiver: I did? When?
M: A couple of days ago. That was not okay.
Caregiver: I'm sorry, buddy. I don't remember doing that.
M: You did. I was upset, you pinched me on my arm, and it hurt. It made me cry. That is not okay. Don't do that again.
Caregiver: Of course, buddy. I'm sorry. I really don't remember that.
M: I do. So don't do that again. It wasn't nice.
Caregiver: Okay, I won't do that again. I'm sorry.

Most adults I know could not have this conversation with their partner, friend, or co-worker, much less someone in a position of power, authority, and control over them, with a 6-year-old brain.

My jaw dropped, my heart swelled, and a big smile spread across my face. I know that this person didn't intend to hurt him, and it was not something I needed to step into. And now, I knew that "M" had the self-love, strength, and emotional skills to communicate and reinforce a healthy boundary despite multiple disabilities. He also felt safe enough to do it. He also told Tutti and me about the incident, which is exactly what we taught him: Tell a trusted adult. I know what that means for him and his life. I know how incredible it is for him to be demonstrating these skills at such a young age, with the conditions and challenges he has. Wow. That is true triumph.

The triumph is in me doing my job for the Hive. We have an interdependence. It's growing, and I can't let them down. We've really been through it all together: births, deaths, divorce, marriage, health scares, jobs, moves, relationships, kids. Horrific events and fucked-up thinking that only survivors really understand. All the things in life that have an impact on us and those around us. We have so much more critically important work in front of us to do. Time to double down on giving back.

The triumph is in the internal healing, being able to move forward with purpose and meaning.

CONCLUSION

"You don't have to see the whole staircase, just take the first step."
–Martin Luther King, Jr.

I hope you've gained insights, cracked a few smiles, and picked up some tools along this journey. You now have access to a growing set of tools and resources that will help you as you continue on your own path.

Some of you who are not survivors might have more questions than answers. You might have some judgments. You might be skeptical about all of this. It's okay. I understand you might have a myriad of reactions to this content and tone. Or you might be wondering what that means to you. What do you do when your partner, child, friend, co-worker, employee, parishioner, community member, or someone important to you is a victim, survivor, or somewhere in between? How do you respond when you see certain things? What is the line, and how do you walk it? Those are really important questions to ask yourself, and learning how to navigate them is crucial.

Reading about others' experiences, such as in this book, is a great first step. More guidance on that topic will be coming soon. In the interim, don't hesitate to reach out—we can help. If you're facing the kinds of challenges described in this book, you have my deepest sympathy. I know how difficult they are to navigate. Thank you for caring enough to do that work. Thank you to those who helped me through mine.

This week marked the first board meeting for HiveStrong and the completion of the major book development work. A painful surgery and recovery gave me the gift of being stationary with a cathartic writing exercise, deadline, and need for productivity, which are key drivers in that accomplishment. Everything can be fuel; each part is a step forward.

The hive has been swarming all around me; the boys are smiling brightly, and we are expanding and growing in our reach. We've figured out our niche and the unique economic empowerment opportunities we can create for survivors. We can taste the very tangible impact we can make in others' lives. We are taking things up a level. There is a very strong pull for what we offer at HiveStrong. Momentum building. Here we go.

Thank you for taking the time to read this. Thank you for going through the journey with me, looking at the fire, looking at the darkness, finding the light, and considering the concepts. Most of all, thank you for contributing to HiveStrong. You have made a difference by showing someone that you care.

Reader Reflection and Journaling

Now it's time to reflect on this last stage, "Purpose."

Journal Exercise

- Where are you on your journey?

  _____

  _____

  _____

  _____

  _____

  _____

- What are the key insights you've gained?

  _____

  _____

  _____

  _____

  _____

  _____

- What tools resonate the most?

_____

_____

_____

_____

_____

_____

We are here to walk alongside you.

You are not alone, and you are enough, I promise.

THANK YOU FOR READING MY BOOK!

JOIN THE COMMUNITY!

Free resources, tools, upcoming free events, and opportunities to engage with the community and founder.

Visit:

I appreciate your interest in my book and value your feedback as it helps me improve future versions of this book. I would appreciate it if you could leave your invaluable review on Amazon.com with your feedback. Thank you!

www.ingramcontent.com/pod-product-compliance
Lightning Source LLC
Chambersburg PA
CBHW020200090426
42734CB00008B/891